Who Do You Belong To?

Mary Monaghan

TORTOISE
PRESS

First published in 2010 by Tortoise Press,
P O Box 163 Melkbosstrand 7437 South Africa
www.marymonaghan.com

ISBN : 978-0-620-47034-6

©2010 Mary Monaghan

Edited by : Jennifer Woodhull
Design and typesetting: Nicole de Swardt
Cover design by: Osnat
Printed and bound by: Craft Print

For Kathryn, Annie, and my parents, who have always allowed me to be true to myself, as they have always been true to me.

Acknowledgements

So many special people have been part of my story and continuing journey, providing words of encouragement and wisdom. To my friends, so many of whom appear in my story, thank you for your unfailing love and support. Your friendship enriches my life. Special thanks to Liam Horan in Ireland; Anna and Nigel in England; Judi Moreo and Liam O'Brien in the United States; Deirdre, Lynn, Pam, and Peter in Johannesburg; Margaret in Port Alfred; and Ann, Cheryl, Diane, Gerald, Jean, Jenny, Joan, Linda, Nicky, Terry, and Yvette in Cape Town.

Thanks to my caring and nurturing editor, Jennifer Woodhull; and to Anne Schuster, whose writing workshops provided the framework for my writing. I also thank my "thinking partner" and writing buddy, Bridgett Whyte, who always allowed me time to think and who patiently helped and supported me through the writing process.

Sharing my story has brought me closer to several members of my family, particularly Ann, George, Marian, and Shelagh in London; and Annie and Mary in Ireland.

My sister, Kathryn, never fails to be there for me. I am blessed to have her unwavering love and support.

Table of Contents

 Introduction

In 2006 I published my first book, *Remember Me?* It told the story of the search for my husband, John, who had left our seemingly perfect marriage to go backpacking for three months in Australia, only to vanish without trace.

John and I are Irish; he from Co. Donegal and my parents were from Co. Mayo. I met him at the Galtymore Irish Club in Cricklewood in 1980; it was a meeting place for the Irish in that part of northwest London, a real institution holding regular dances with Irish show bands. It was on Cricklewood Broadway, a noisy road, always busy no matter what time of the day or night. The Galtymore took up almost a whole block; its big display board, edged in green, announced the show bands playing over the weekend. Burly bouncers glowered at you as you made your way inside to the dimly lit dance floor. I was instantly bowled over by John's good looks and easy charm when I met him there. He was tall, fresh faced, with an easy smile. He was seventeen at the time and I was twenty-three.

I followed John to South Africa a few years later, after he made the decision to go there to seek his fortune. We led a happy life, socialising with a group of mostly Irish friends, loving the sunshine and the wide open spaces, making frequent trips to the bush (South Africa's wild country). We married in 1985, buying a house in the suburbs complete with pool and guest cottages. We had the perfect life, a happy marriage, a thriving business, great friends; money was plentiful. I loved living there in a cottagey house with a sparkling blue pool. The sun shone brightly on my life.

In December 1992 John told me that his business was in difficulties. He had decided to close it down, go backpacking in Australia for three months, and then start a new venture on his return, renovating old houses. I remember going into the garden after he told me of his decision, walking round and round aimlessly, hardly noticing the roses that were in full bloom or the bees sipping at their nectar. I tried to make sense of it all, how could he just make this decision without including me? It wasn't right! Despite the brilliant sunshine I felt a darkness grip my heart.

John was very stressed, on edge and snappy before he left. Simple things like too much sugar in his coffee brought him over the edge, smashing his mug in the sink in his haste to pour it away. I decided to be supportive and helped him with all his preparations. I waved him off as his friend Nigel took him to the airport. John had convinced me that he would rather say goodbye to me at home than have a tearful public goodbye at the airport.

Nigel was from Cork. A plumber by trade, he was John's best friend and they were inseparable. He was a great friend to me always and John had tasked him to be my "minder" in the time he was away, making sure that I had someone to help me while I was on my own.

As I left for work that day, leaving John behind at the house, knowing that I would not see him for the three months he would be away, my hands shook as I gripped the steering wheel. I edged along in the traffic, reacting absentmindedly to the cars hooting at me to move it along and stop dawdling.

The agreement was for us to have minimal contact, as John would be in a remote area of Australia. In the three months after he left, I became aware of the extent of his financial problems. I was forced to sell our beautiful house, and the proceeds were attached. I had already bought a rundown house in a rough neighbourhood, with rotting floorboards and crumbling window frames, and now had no money to do it up. The house became like a prison to me. I was too ashamed of its dinginess to invite my friends to visit me there.

Still there was no word from John. I tried to keep my head above water by raising chickens on the farm we owned outside Magaliesburg, just over an hour's drive from Johannesburg. It had been on the market for months but there were no offers to buy it. I was battling. My friends were becoming increasingly worried about me, as was my sister, Kathryn, who was a teacher in London and had known John from the days when we had first started going out. I tried to downplay the extent of my financial woes, not wanting to worry her.

From time to time I heard from John's parents, who had also had no contact from him. John's aunt Elizabeth was particularly concerned, and phoned me regularly to see if I was doing all right. She had been close to John and me when we had all been living in London, often going out to pubs and clubs with us. No one could understand why John had disappeared. It was a mystery to all of us. I tried to enrol the help of private investigators and Interpol to search for John, but with no success. I was at my wits' end as year after year went by with no word from him.

My situation improved when I landed a good job with Gilbey's as Customer Financial Services Manager, responsible for credit control. A job of increased responsibility and much pressure, it helped divert my attention from John, keeping me busy as I reinvented myself as a person in my own right. I was now in an environment where people didn't really know my story and accepted me for who I was.

Four years after John had left, I decided to seek a divorce and annulment through the Catholic Church. It was a tough decision to make; I was reluctant to accept that our marriage was over. Night after night I wandered around the house talking to myself, trying desperately to make sense of it all and to convince myself that I needed to move on. My decision was affirmed when Nigel confirmed many years later that John had left for Australia with another woman, Tamsyn, an Australian girl he had met when he was working on a contract in Richards Bay. The granting of the annulment helped me to move on with my life but I never gave up my quest to find John, there were just too many unanswered questions.

I was transferred from Johannesburg to Cape Town and was able to live in a house I had designed and built in Grotto Bay, on the Cape West Coast. It was my version of an Irish cottage, exactly the way I wanted it to be: rough plastered walls, full of nooks and crannies, with a green roof. It was a symbol of new beginnings for me. I rebuilt my life there. It calmed me to sit on the veranda night after night, watching the sun set over the bay, then staying there as the first stars came out, closing my eyes and listening to the waves.

I loved my job, enjoying my new life in the Cape; but the mystery of John's disappearance never stopped haunting me. Close to Christmas 1998 I had a call from Elizabeth, John's aunt. She had been trying to find an address or phone number for him since 1997, the year in which contact was finally made with his parents. They made the decision not to give the details to me, but Elizabeth vowed to help me. A year later she succeeded in bringing my search for him to an end and finding answers to my questions. Almost six years after John had left for Australia I made contact with him. My first words over the phone were: 'Remember me?'

As a result of writing the book of my story, my life moved in new directions and took unexpected turns. *Who Do You Belong To?* continues the story of my journey.

As the first chapter reveals, my quest was strongly influenced by the discovery of a journal written by my mother shortly before her death. I have used brief excerpts from this journal to introduce each subsequent chapter.

Also by Mary Monaghan
Remember Me?
Tortoise Press
ISBN: 978-0-620-36648-9

Chapter 1
Green Are the Hills Far Away

Poem to Mother

Vibrant, sparkling, bright, flowing
She sparkles as the stream that flows by
Constant, soothing, tranquil, peaceful

She flows in and out of my life, watching over me
Helping me be all that I can be
Vibrant, sparkling, bright, flowing

Run with your life as it carries you in its flow
Do not be afraid, be true to yourself
Constant, soothing, tranquil, peaceful

Her soothing murmur calming me
Her passion encouraging me
Vibrant, sparkling, bright, flowing

She flows on, eternally inquisitive
Awakening in me a sense of possibilities
Constant, soothing, tranquil, peaceful

Embrace all that life offers you
Her light shining on the water
Vibrant, sparkling, bright, flowing
Constant, soothing, tranquil, peaceful

'Where did you put the suitcase with all the old photos?' I asked my sister, Kathryn, as we sat in her flat one Sunday morning in May 2005. It was a chilly, grey day in London and rain was drumming against the sash windows. It was good to be inside. Why was I always surprised by the cold when I visited from South Africa? I should have known better, having spent years of my childhood and early adult life in England ... 'I'm sure it's in the attic', Kathryn said. 'I've tried to batch the photos in envelopes; they'll be easier to sort through that way.'

I found the old-fashioned brown suitcase with its rusted, battered hinges at the back of the attic and passed it down to Kathryn, who put it on the settee. She went into the kitchen to make coffee. 'This should warm us up', she said. 'We've got loads of time, we only need to be at the Pink Rupee at seven o'clock.' We'd arranged to meet up with friends and family for an Indian dinner at our favourite restaurant in Cricklewood. It was a standing arrangement whenever I was over from South Africa; it was an easy way to catch up with everybody.

I knelt on the carpet and took a deep breath before opening up the suitcase. The particular photos I was looking for were from Cyprus. I hoped that they would bring back memories of a moment I was writing about in my book, *Remember Me?* which was nearing completion at last.

Once I'd started sifting through the photos my parents had accumulated over the years, it was hard to stop. As I opened the old albums and untied ribbons around packets of letters, our childhood and my parents' life together began to unfold before my eyes. In amongst the bundles at the bottom of the suitcase I saw a yellowing exercise book, RAF issue. It was filled with my mother's expressive handwriting. At the top of the first page she had written the title, *Green Are the Hills Far Away.*

Intrigued, I moved over to the armchair and placed my coffee mug beside me. In a nest of plump cushions, with my feet curled up beneath me, I opened the exercise book and started to read my mother's story.

I am writing this story for you, Kathryn and Mary, from Johannesburg in 1988 where I'm visiting Mary and John. I'm getting old now and I want you to know about my early life in Ireland.

I know I haven't spoken to you much about my childhood; it has always been a bit of a sore subject with me. It was such an unhappy period of my life, but I think the time has come to explain to you why I have always been so reluctant to go home to Ballinrobe. It holds bad memories for me.

My father died of consumption six weeks after I was born in 1917, leaving my mother to bring up my sister Marie and I single-handedly. He had been in the sanatorium for six months before he died; consumption was rife in Ireland in those days. He had worked in a draper's shop and earned enough to keep the family in food and shelter; there was no need for my mother to work. Now here she was with very little money, two small children and a small widow's pension. She always considered herself as being from the better part of town, living as she did on High Street, and she hated the thought of having to earn a living. But the reality was that she had to generate some form of income, so she begrudgingly took to dressmaking and doing alterations for people in the town. She kicked against it, always considering herself to be above this, preferring to think of it simply as a service she was providing for her friends.

From my early childhood she always made it clear that Marie was her favourite, the intellectual of the family. No chance of Marie being sent to the well to get water every evening. She couldn't be parted from her studies. That duty always fell to me. The bucket was heavy to carry and I was scolded if I spilled too much on the climb back up the hill.

'You'll never make anything of yourself', my mother said to me. 'You'll come to no good ... Marie is such a lovely, sweet child. I don't know where you came from. We would all be better off if you had never been born.' So continued my mother's almost daily refrain. I couldn't understand why both she and the nuns [at school] were so heartless. They were supposed to be holy people; my mother went to Mass every day and was a pillar of the church. How could she spend her life abusing me like this? Even as a child I realised that there was a contradiction between her fervent faith and the hand raised to beat me at every opportunity. And all under the gaze of the myriad of statues of Our Lady.

I turned to Kathryn who had been listening intently as I read aloud. 'I knew she wasn't keen on going back to Ballinrobe but I had no idea how rough life was for her there', I mused.

'I know—it struck me too when I read her journal', Kathryn replied. 'That must be why she was always so careful to treat us both equally, never showing favouritism. It makes sense now; she took it to the other extreme, keeping things so impartial. Do you remember her favourite saying: "You are no better than anyone else and no one is any better than you"?'

'How could I forget it? It's something that has stayed with me always', I said, gazing out at the grey skyline. 'It has helped me to get past what happened with John, I know I deserved better and that I will survive. There's no point letting what has happened in the past ruin my future, I refuse to become bitter and twisted. She got on with her life and so will I.'

The rain still falling steadily, I read on:

'Kathleen O'Toole, come up to the front of the class!' was a common refrain from the nuns at school. I had misbehaved yet again and had to take my punishment ...

We were beaten with a black belt the nuns wore around their waists and when ... older, with a wooden slapper. One day I took the slapper from the nun's desk, broke it and put it in the dry toilet.

One day the circus was in town, I knew I would be kept in while the rest of the school would be going to the matinee, because I couldn't do my garment (mauve). I decided to play truant, or mitch as we called it. I left the house and was just going around the river when Nora O'Malley who lived near us came on the scene. I literally dragged her crying with me. We went up the green and hid in the burnt out army barracks. Unfortunately I peeped out and a woman called Dandy Biddy saw me.

The next morning the bell was rung. I was marched to Our Lady's statue on the grand stairs and my green ribbon was taken off me. My green ribbon, the one got before we became a Child of Mary. The Reverend Mother slapped me across the face and said to me 'What boys were in the barracks?' Boys hadn't even entered my head. I was only 12. Also she said, 'Why aren't you like your sister Marie, never gives the nuns any trouble, Nora O'Malley wouldn't have played truant if it wasn't for you.'

I thought, as I'm so bad I might as well give them as much trouble as I can. So when someone gave me an autograph book I wrote there, 'love none, trust few, always paddle your own canoe.' Of course Sister Margaret Mary caught me in front of the whole school. I was marched again this time to the kitchen to burn the book because I had written the word 'love.'

'She always made light of her rebelliousness, it must have been awful for her at school … Do you remember the story of the nuns' long johns?' Kathryn nodded, handing me another cup of coffee. 'She writes about it here', I said. 'Listen.'

Part of the curriculum was domestic science. So what did that entail? Why doing the nuns' laundry of course! We stood in the basement of the convent swirling their long johns and bodices around in steaming vats of water, our hands red and burning from the harsh detergent. One day it got too much for me and when time came to iron their undergarments I decided to starch their long johns and stand them to attention along the passage. You can imagine the response that evoked. Kathleen O'Toole beaten mercilessly with the strap again, not to mention the hiding from my mother when I got home.

'She was always such a rebel, wasn't she?' Kathryn said. 'Fred [my pet name for our father] was always the quiet one.' I had started calling my father, whose name was Paddy, by the name of Fred when I became a teenager. I suppose it was my way of showing that I was growing up, I felt uncomfortable calling him Daddy. He didn't object to it and would look at me with his soft smile when I called him Fred. He was a gentle, patient man. I remember my mother at a function at the army base in Oakington in the late 1970s, coming outside to see the sergeant major's hat and gloves laid neatly on a table. Memories from her childhood of the Black and Tans in Ireland came back to her and she promptly put the hat and gloves on the floor and proceeded to dance on them before my father ushered her out quickly, a smile on his face.

'Mother must have been quite something with the boys', I replied, grinning.

1943

I went to the usual Sunday night hop [Mother's journal continued] *at Gannon's Maple Ballroom in December 1943, as I always seemed to be bored with Ballinrobe life. The usual gang was there: Dan and Josie Loughrey, the Gannon's. Nancy was married by then. It was a very dull night until Wilson Jennings (he owned a pub on Bowgate St.) bet Paddy he wouldn't kiss me. They all got in a circle; he went to run away. I grabbed him and kissed him!*

You may wonder, as I didn't know him well. He never danced and only came to the hall when the pubs were shut. But Wilson had said if he kissed me he could have two free pints. I knew he was unemployed and I thought, why not? That's how our romance began.

He was so shy he hid afterwards for a few weeks. That was fatal for him seeing what I am like. I waylaid him up the town and he hadn't a chance! One night after the dance he asked could he walk me home as far as the Mill Bridge. All hell broke loose when the romance was discovered. I was locked in, beaten. My Uncle Peter refused to let Paddy in to the Town Hall dances. He had to wait outside until the dance was over. Uncle Peter was secretary of the Town Hall.

Mother told me if I gave Paddy up she would give me a cottage and land on Creagh Road; when I refused she went to Fitzgerald solicitors and left it all to the Chinese missions.

Wedding photo 1947

Round the Bowers in Ballinrobe

Despite my mother's difficult upbringing, she and my father had given us such a stable and happy family life. Her love for my father was a constant theme through her journal:

Paddy was so different from all the rest I flirted with. I was lucky he was so kind, gentle and understanding of all my moods and capers. I felt at peace when I was with him and safe.

After all the hardships of her early life in Ireland, my mother was indeed lucky to have known the enduring love of a good man. I had expected the same, but after twelve years of being with John, life turned out so very differently. I couldn't understand why he didn't return from his three-month trip to Australia. He just had to come back. I battled financially, searching for him constantly.

It had been nine months now, and as Christmas approached I travelled to the airport to meet the weekly flight from Australia, believing that he would come back. I was dressed up for the occasion, wanting to surprise him, only to ruin my make-up as I ran crying to the Ladies each week when I realised he wasn't on the plane. I had taken out Australian visas in case private investigators were able to track him down and I would need to travel to Australia at short notice. They'd expire and I'd renew them, never giving up hope. I felt so very alone. My mother must have felt similarly lonely when my father died. I cried softly as I read on.

Since 29th July 1984 life is just one day at a time. There are times that I wouldn't be able to carry on but I know he's around somewhere, helping me along like he always did in his quiet, good-humoured way—Just waiting—Paddy.

I have had a very good life: a wonderful husband, two daughters that never gave me a minute's worry loved them both equally. They have been so good to Paddy and I, gave us everything they possibly could and more. I hope they'll forgive me if I sometimes did things 'my way'. Just remember, I used to be known as 'the red one on the hill'. I hope you both will too always be true to yourselves.

I shivered, suddenly cold; it was as if I were reading a message from the grave. By writing my story I was indeed "being true to myself". My book was going to be my story pure and simple, with no recriminations, no bitterness: just simply a record of how life had been for me and how I had overcome the obstacles put in my way. My mother had given me self-confidence, the ability to understand that I was indeed as good as anyone else and that no matter what hand I was dealt I would survive. I had been having doubts about writing my book, but Mother's journal gave me the strength to continue. Holding her journal in my hands all these years after her death, I realised how much I owed her. Through writing my own story I knew I would put to rest the bleakest period in my life.

I looked up. The rain had stopped and it was time to get ready for our outing to the Pink Rupee. I closed *Green Are the Hills Far Away* and placed it carefully in the old leather suitcase. It was so opportune that I had had the chance to read the journal now; the words of my mother served to give me the confidence they had always given me to do the best I could. I knew my parents would be proud of the journey I had undertaken since the disappearance of John. I must not disappoint them. I wanted them to be proud of the person I had become.

Chapter 2
When I Was a Child ...

I had to look Cyprus up on the map; I had never heard of it.

My trip to London had surfaced so many memories, it was good to get back to my house in Grotto Bay. I so loved being there, spending hours looking at the waves crashing on the rocks, watching the sun set over Dassen Island. I loved the wildness of the Cape West Coast, so similar in many ways to the west of Ireland: it had a rugged and dangerous beauty, a sense of danger and desolation.

I was never sure where I felt most at home. My family roots were in Ireland but I had never lived there. I had spent so much of my childhood in England, but somehow never felt that it was home, despite many happy memories of my time there. Ballinrobe, Ireland would always be home to me. I had spent most of my adult life in South Africa but when I was in Cape Town I felt my "Irishness" very keenly. In many ways it was good to be rooted in two places, and between the Cape and Ballinrobe I was able to find calmness always. They were the two places that centred me and to which I always returned no matter where I travelled.

I caught the smell of jasmine from my neighbour's garden as I sat on the veranda in Grotto Bay one warm summer evening, and my thoughts drifted to Cyprus and memories of my time there. I recalled that charmed time of my childhood in the 1960s: the smell of oranges and lemons, the dry, dusty fields, the goats on the mountainside. It was a wonderful period: school in the morning, the pool or the beach in the afternoon. I loved the heat and the outdoor life. Kathryn and my mother had not been so happy in the hot weather, but my father and I had revelled in it, becoming brown as berries.

Kathryn and I always felt safe, even though the Greeks and Turks were engaged in civil war. The day I went to make my First Holy Communion we were stopped at a checkpoint by soldiers wielding guns, and we had to get out while they searched the car. I could remember my mother fussing over my dress and veil as we waited in the hot sun. Guns and military checkpoints were the order of the day, but I could remember only love and laughter and warmth.

At some point in my book, I had written about an incident during our stay in Cyprus, and I could visualise the photo that captured it. I was proudly dressed in my Brownie uniform, my face serious, my dolls lined up on the veranda ... My mother loved to tell how I had put my uniform on in response to a radio instruction to RAF personnel to remain in uniform at all times, and how I had refused to remove mine until the "all clear" had been given.

It was a sixteen-mile drive from our house in Nicosia through two Greek and four Turkish checkpoints to Kyrenia, but the journey was always worth it. The attitude of the soldiers at both checkpoints varied from day to day. At times they were polite, asking my father for his driver's licence and then casting a cursory glance inside the car. Sometimes we weren't as lucky. Machine guns were pointed at us and we were abruptly told to get out of the car and stand at the side of the road. I remember standing there for what seemed an age under the hot midday sun, squinting as the glare dazzled my eyes, seeing just enough to be mortified as the soldier rifled through my beach bag, shaking out my towel and watching my underwear fall to the ground. I blushed, my face beetroot red; a six-year-old girl having a soldier see such personal things. My mother put her hand on my shoulder and smiled reassuringly, attempting to comfort me.

When we got to the beach we'd paddle in the sea for hours on end, play on the sand, and enjoy the never-ending sunshine. As the day drew to a close we'd sleep in our tent, worn out from the sea and the sun, dozing to the sound of the waves lapping against the rocks and the gentle chatter of our parents' conversation. Even when times were unstable we made the trip, often driving in convoy behind three-ton trucks. I was never scared, even when someone closely resembling Che Guevara came out of the bushes on the mountainside brandishing his gun and demanding cigarettes. He was bearded and unkempt, dressed in camouflage gear, spitting out instructions to us. By rights I should have been terrified but my parents stayed calm, did what he asked, and carried on as if nothing had happened. It was just part of daily life for us.

My father always made light of any security concerns and he refused to allow them to interfere with his life. The first Christmas that we were in Cyprus in 1963, tensions between Greek and Turkish Cypriots were running high. My mother would hurry us indoors from the garden, fearful for our safety as we watched Turkish planes fly menacingly overhead on missions deeper into the island. We were confined to base to avoid encountering any fighting in town; our area was secure but our safety couldn't be guaranteed if we went there.

We had basic supplies available on the base at the NAAFI store but no turkeys were in stock there. My mother had bought a chicken for Christmas Day, it was the best she could do. On Christmas Eve she busied herself in the kitchen, the radio tuned in to the British Forces Broadcasting Service, our lifeline to home. As three o'clock approached she turned up the volume, "Carols from Kings" was due on. When the service started we sang along with the hymns. That always brought us back to our previous Christmases in the heart of an English winter, so different from the one we were experiencing now. No fire blazed in the hearth, no scarves and gloves necessary if we went outside.

As the carol concert continued, Kathryn and I helped with the preparations for Christmas Day. We handed mother tins of canned fruit for the trifle, opened the packets of special trifle biscuits. Kathryn prepared the jelly and monitored carefully the amount of sherry being added to the trifle, too much and she would refuse to eat it. We might be in different surroundings this year but everything was as it always was, except for the scrawny chicken instead of the turkey of course.

Mother started to look anxiously at the kitchen clock. 'Where can your father be?' she said. 'He was supposed to finish work at two o'clock and now it is almost four o'clock, where can he be?' It was unlike my father to be late—he was always such a creature of habit, totally reliable. As the concert finished we went out to the washing line in the garden, Kathryn helping my mother unpeg the washing and me, still too short to reach the line, holding out the peg bag to make sure all the pegs were safely stored. The washing had dried well in the warm sunshine, now everything would be clean and fresh for Christmas Day.

St. Patrick's Day in Cyprus

Just as we were packing the last of the washing in the basket my father arrived, his Land Rover screeching to a halt in the driveway. He leapt out of the car, grabbed a large brown parcel from the passenger's seat and held it up triumphantly. 'I've got us a turkey!' he exclaimed.

'Where on earth did you get it from?' my mother asked, dropping the washing basket.

'From town, of course. We couldn't have Christmas without a turkey.'

'But that's so dangerous! We're not supposed to go into town!'

My father gave my mother one of his quiet smiles. 'It wasn't too bad, I steered clear of most of the shooting. I couldn't disappoint the girls, what would Christmas be like for them without a turkey?'

My mother smiled back at him, relieved that he was OK. Indeed, what would Christmas be like without a turkey? My father was a quiet man but a determined one nonetheless, and knew what he wanted. The turkey we had the next day tasted better than ever.

Kathryn and I went on a trip to Cyprus in 1989, the year after our mother died. I hadn't been back there for over twenty years. Kathryn suggested it and John encouraged me to go. It had been a tough year for me. Despite living so far away from my parents for so many years, now that they were both no longer there I felt like an orphan, totally alone. Kathryn and I had grown apart after I moved to South Africa. This would be an opportunity to reconnect.

Cyprus was as beautiful as I remembered it. It was springtime, so poppies were out in the fields and the sea sparkled. At last I started to relax and unwind. Since my mother's death I had been stressed, on edge, I couldn't settle to anything. Now that I was back in Cyprus the familiar setting of my happy childhood served to comfort me and calm me.

While we were in Nicosia we visited friends of my parents, the Fishers, a Hungarian couple they had met when they first lived in Cyprus in the early 1950s. They were mentioned in Mother's journal:

Elsa and Sanya Fisher lived near us. She was a Rumanian Jew and he a Hungarian Jew. They were in Baghdad on their honeymoon when war broke out. They couldn't go back and drifted to Cyprus where he started the first photographic shop on the island. I met a lot of different nationalities with them at their musical evenings.

My parents had remained firm friends with the Fishers through the years, and they were very kind to me and Kathryn when we lived in Cyprus in the '60s. They gave us presents of books and even traditional paintings, which we have to this day.

After a few days in Cyprus, Elsa Fisher took us to one side. 'You know my story', she said. 'I lost all my family in the war when Sanya and I were away on honeymoon. We lived the rest of our lives with just each other, no family. Remember you are all you both have left. You have the opportunity to be family together—don't lose that, it is a gift you should cherish.'

Kathryn and I looked at each other. She was right; we had only each other now and we had to acknowledge that and embrace it. From that day our relationship changed. The words of a wise woman who had suffered so much from the loss of her loved ones had awakened us to the importance of family.

Shortly before I was due to fly back to South Africa, John phoned. He was very quiet and subdued on the phone, which I took to be a sign of exhaustion after his hiking trip in the mountains. In hindsight it was probably sheepishness, because it heralded the start of his infidelity. It was on this trip that he met Tracey, who later became his girlfriend and lived with him while he was on one of his extended contracts in Richards Bay. There he began to live a double life. He later betrayed both Tracey and me with Tamsyn, the woman with whom he started a new life in Australia.

Chapter 3
Who Do You Belong To?

She opened the window and threw a bucket of water over him.

My early married days in the late 1980s were filled with parties and socialising, the Irish community in Johannesburg enjoyed a good party. One memorable party was at Joan's house in Ferndale, a leafy suburb of Johannesburg. Joan and I had been friends since she had arrived in South Africa from Ireland in 1985. She was from Kerry, working for a packaging company in their human resources department. She was close to me in age, lively and full of fun. We stood in the kitchen at her party that summer's evening. The recent thunderstorm had cooled things off, so it was pleasantly balmy. Most of the women had gathered in the lounge area, sitting in huddles; the majority of them were married with children, happily discussing domestic things. Joan and I, although married, had no children, so discussions around schoolchildren's clothes etc. were of little interest to us.

It was calm in the kitchen; we could at least hear each other talk. We had moved there to grab some wine and to chat. We both had demanding jobs and hadn't managed to meet

Wedding day, 1985

for dinner for some time. We chatted away easily about the pressures of work, impossible deadlines, etc., watching as people came in and out helping themselves to drinks and snacks. There was a constant flow of people who greeted us as they moved past, not engaging with us as they could see we were happy with our own company. The smell of the meat being grilled outside in the garden wafted into the house. My tummy rumbled, I was starting to get peckish.

Early days

Just as I was thinking of grabbing some food one man decided to stop and talk to us. I had seen him before; he was from Donegal, older than us, a short, portly, grey-haired man in his sixties. I didn't know his name but knew him by sight. He knew Joan well and spoke to her for a while before turning to me. 'And you? What's your name?'

'Mary', I replied (not very helpful in an Irish gathering as there were always a lot of Marys).

He looked me up and down. 'And who do you belong to?'

I was taken aback and didn't answer. He repeated the question. 'And who do you belong to? You are married aren't you?'

'Yes, I am married to John Monaghan, but I don't belong to him.'

'John the painter, that's who you belong to.' He smiled, turned on his heel and walked away.

I was speechless; to think I only had value in terms of who I was married to! It gave me a clear idea of the way many men saw the world. Well, I didn't belong to anyone, I never would, and I vowed to make sure that I would not compromise on this ever in my life. I was no one's possession. Part of my journey after John left has been to become more of a survivor, far less vulnerable and dependent, someone to be valued for who she is and most certainly not for who she "belongs to". The journey hasn't been easy, and I have been confronted along the way by arrogant men who feel threatened by single women.

This incident reminded me of one that had shaken me shortly after John had gone away to Australia in 1993.

'What do you think you will sing?' my friend and colleague Deirdre asked as we set off for a karaoke evening. We had worked together for several years now. Deirdre was younger than I, Afrikaans, with a positive attitude to life, always with a cheery smile.

'Nothing if I can help it', I replied. 'I can't sing to save my life, I intend to keep a low profile and let everyone else do their thing. We've got our fair share of exhibitionists, so we won't be short of volunteers.'

We continued to drive through the streets of Braamfontein. It was a business area of Johannesburg, somewhat run down and not the place to linger about on your own after nightfall, as it quickly became deserted, just a few hobos wandering around checking the contents of the dustbins. I had now been promoted to the position of manager of customer services for both Nedbank Visa and MasterCard in addition to American Express Card. It was a pressurised and busy position; I had over fifty staff in my team. I had organised a karaoke evening as a teambuilding exercise. Most of the staff jumped at the chance to join in; they were invited together with their partners, it promised to be a fun evening.

Gary had gone ahead to check that everything was set up. He was one of the supervisors and played in a band, so if anyone knew how to set things up stage- and sound-wise, it was him. He held a senior position in the department and took his job very seriously; it was hard to reconcile this corporate image of him with his on-stage persona, when he played bass in a heavy rock band, a favourite with "head bangers".

Deirdre and I were early so we just found ourselves a table in the corner, ordered drinks from the bar, and waited for the rest of the gang to arrive. They were coming straight from work so they mostly came together. The venue soon became crowded, the noise level became higher and higher, people who saw each other all day and now were seeing each other again and still had so much to talk about. We had a good team, young and old, mostly female but with some males thrown in for good measure. Traditionally, customer service departments were staffed by women, but it was good to have a few men there too. I had tried to balance the male/female mix to ensure a diversity of personalities and backgrounds to better reflect the client base with whom we were dealing.

Gary started up the karaoke, people were queuing to go up. I was amazed to see some of our quieter staff take to it like ducks to water. Not only did they sing but they did the actions too and brought the house down.

'Come on, I've chosen a song for you', Gary said. 'You've got to lead by example; you are the manager after all.'

'No I can't', I said, 'I sing so badly, everyone will leave the room.'

'Too bad', he replied, and led me to the stage. I was sure no one had any idea of how bad my singing skills were; if they had they would definitely have kept me far away from the stage. I jumped up on the stage as the music started to play "It's My Party and I'll Cry if I Want To". Great, well here goes. I felt my colour rise as I started to sing, out of tune as usual. I could see the look of horror on people's faces as they realised I wasn't kidding, I was bad. I tried to move to the music but my legs were leaden, I was so very uncomfortable, I felt my heart was going to explode. This was supposed to be fun, not stressful.

Gary took pity on me and got everyone to join in. The song seemed never ending but eventually it finished and I beat a hasty retreat to my table. Deirdre held out a glass of wine to me. 'I think you might need this', she said, grinning.

'That's for sure, never again', I replied, plonking myself down in my chair, thankful that no one in their right mind would ask me to do any more singing. It was a successful evening, relaxed, full of fun, everyone was enjoying themselves whether they sang or not.

'I'm on my way', I said to Gary as I moved to the door.

One of my staff came over to me; he was in his late twenties, medium height and build, with sandy coloured hair.

'Would you mind giving me a lift home?' he asked. 'You pass my way and my wife has already gone home.'

'Of course', I replied. 'I'm sure she is tired with being pregnant. When is the baby due?'

'Still three months to go', he replied.

We got in the car and drove the fifteen minutes to his place, chatting about the events of the evening. I stopped the car in the parking lot outside his house but he made no move to get out. I looked over to his house; it was in darkness, no lights left on for him. The garden was neat, a recently mowed lawn and well tended flower beds, all that was missing was the picket fence. He leaned over to me. 'It must be lonely for you with John away', he said. 'You shouldn't be on your own, a woman has needs, I could help you with that.'

I couldn't believe what I was hearing. He worked for me, he was far younger than I, he was married with a pregnant wife, and yet he was coming on to me.

'I don't think so', I said sternly.

He looked at me intently. 'You don't know what you are missing, I could make you feel great.'

'Don't be ridiculous, please get out of the car now', I shouted.

'I find women in power such a turn-on, you know you want it.'

'No I don't, get out of this car before I make a scene.'

He looked at me, moved towards me. I knew he was strong, far stronger than I. I suddenly felt incredibly vulnerable; what if he forced himself on me? He would probably be too strong for me. I wouldn't stand a chance.

'Don't you dare', I said. 'Now get out of this car immediately.'

He hesitated. I moved my hand towards the hooter, I was going to press the horn so hard it would wake up the neighbourhood, including his wife. He held my gaze, saw I meant business, and then decided that he had better call it a day. He opened the door.

'Too bad', he said, 'you could do with it, I know', and swaggered off into his house.

I locked the car door, took a few deep breaths, and drove away as fast as I could, tears streaming down my face. I opened the car window just a little, wary of hijackers. I needed air, I was battling to breathe, my pulse was racing. I had done nothing to get myself in this situation; all I was doing was giving a colleague a lift. Why was I subjected to this violation? I realised just how vulnerable I had been and how easily the situation could have soured. I hated the fact that a man could have the ability to be such an aggressor—not only that, but to feel no remorse about it. In some ways he seemed to think that he would be doing me a favour.

Ten minutes later I was home, trembling; I put my keys down on the kitchen table and sat down for a few minutes to gather my thoughts. I couldn't believe what had just happened. I felt so shaky and weak, and now what should I do? Tell everyone and take disciplinary action against this man? What purpose would that serve? It would embarrass his wife; the rest of the male staff would probably want to beat him up. Then of course he would probably say that I had led him along. I decided to rather have a stern talk with him the next day, lay the ground rules and tell him that it had better not happen again.

That is what I did. In hindsight I wish I had been stronger, made more of an issue of it, but I wasn't feeling strong enough to pursue it. I was already feeling off balance after John's disappearance and now this, it was just too much. There is no doubt in my mind that if this were to happen now, the outcome would be different. I would not keep quiet.

My encounters with men in the period after John's disappearance weren't all bad. Not so long after he left one incident helped to boost my confidence.

'Shall we do Gino's tonight after squash?' Deirdre asked. I was looking forward to playing squash with Deirdre; it was our Wednesday night ritual. It was a good way to unwind, get some exercise, burn off some calories, and put them all back on again by going out for Italian afterwards. It helped to keep my mind off my troubles. I needed to be as busy as possible to block out the nagging questions that constantly filled my thoughts: *Where is John? Is he OK?*

We played a good game of squash but spent a fair amount of time chatting and catching up with the latest news. Deirdre and I had worked together at Nedbank Card Division and she followed me when I took on the position of Customer Financial Services Manager at Gilbey's. Gilbey's was a liquor company with its head office in Stellenbosch. I was based in their Johannesburg offices but had to travel to Cape Town frequently for meetings. The senior position I held there helped me get back on my feet after the money problems John had left me with. Deirdre and I were generally so busy that we didn't get too much time to talk about personal things; our squash night was the time we caught up.

It was a bitterly cold winter's evening; we were hot and bothered after the game but needed to wrap up warmly afterwards. We hit the showers and then got dressed for Gino's, our local Italian restaurant. I glanced at my black tracksuit pants and red top. I should start paying a bit more attention to the way I dressed. I know it was after a game of squash but still I needed to look more respectable. We were going out after all. I felt scruffy, unkempt; I knew I had started to let myself go.

It took us just about fifteen minutes to get ready. I added a quick dash of lipstick and then was done. I followed Deirdre to the car park, flung my bag in the boot, and set off for Gino's. My car was registering the outside temperature as four degrees. Despite the cold evening Gino's was packed. It was warm and the smells of pizza, garlic, and good strong Italian coffee filled the air. I had been going there since 1983 when John and I first moved to Mondeor, a Johannesburg suburb close by. Gino greeted me and Deirdre with a big smile and showed us to our table. The waitress arrived soon afterwards and left menus for us. It wasn't necessary to do that; we generally ate exactly the same thing every week, creatures of habit. We added a bottle of wine and some sparkling water and we were all set.

The wine was poured for us and then we settled back for a good chat. The waitress came for our order, then left us to our own devices; she could see we did not want to be disturbed and waited patiently for a gap in our conversation before asking me to taste the wine. I had been in Cape Town for a while attending meetings, so Deirdre and I hadn't had time to connect.

Our conversation was interrupted by a young girl with a ponytail, a short black skirt and bright red top, selling flowers for charity, red roses. Generally she offered to the man at the table but even though we were just two women it seemed she was going to try her luck with us. We both smiled politely and waved her away. She moved on to the next table. She was doing good business tonight, as it seemed she had very few roses left.

About ten minutes later she was back again; this was getting a bit much I thought to myself, we had already said no. She looked up at me and said, 'Please pick a rose'.

'No thank you', I replied.

'There is a gentleman over there who wants to buy you a rose.'

I glanced over at Deirdre, she was grinning at me. I opened and shut my mouth; I didn't know what to say. Rarely am I lost for words but this was one of those occasions.

'He says to tell you that your smile lights up the room.'

My face reflected the red of my sweatshirt. 'Thank you', I stammered.

Deirdre looked at me, a broad smile on her face, relishing this moment. I was battling to handle the situation, it was so unexpected, and I didn't feel equipped to deal with it.

'Please pick a rose', the young woman prompted me.

I chose a rose and regaining some composure, asked her who was offering it to me.

She gestured over to a table in the corner where there were six men.

'Which one?' I whispered.

'The one on the end, with a beard.'

I grinned foolishly; I was handling the situation like a shy schoolgirl, giggly and embarrassed. Looking down, I gathered some composure and smiled over at him. He acknowledged with a smile and a nod of his head.

I tried to concentrate on my conversation with Deirdre but it was a tall order. We were both giggling, totally taken by surprise, and trying to handle the situation as gracefully as possible. It wasn't working; any attempt at normal conversation had gone out of the window. I felt myself getting hotter and hotter. I felt embarrassed, excited, and nervous all at the same time.

'Wow, that is just so incredible', Deirdre said.

'I know, can you imagine, what a lovely thing to do!'

'You're going to have to go over and thank him.'

'I can't.'

'Yes you can, it would be rude not to.'

And so the conversation went on for the next ten minutes. I tried to calm down sufficiently and get back to a face that was a paler shade of beetroot before summoning up enough courage to thank my admirer.

'Go on', Deirdre said, 'just go and thank him on your way to the loo. If you wait much longer he will be gone.'

'Just give me another couple of minutes.'

I wished that I looked calmer than I felt. Trying to look as casual and composed as possible I headed over to the table.

I smiled at him as I approached, and said, 'Thanks for the rose'.

'It's my pleasure', he replied.

I went to the Ladies, splashed some water on my face, and went back to join Deirdre at the table.

'What did he say?' she asked.

'He said it was a pleasure.'

'As simple as that.'

'Yes, as simple as that.'

'He didn't ask you for your phone number?'

'No, he didn't, that's what was so nice. It was a table full of guys but they were very respectful, just having a quiet meal together. They weren't drunk or funny with me, just decent people.'

We carried on chatting for some time, marvelling at the fact that this had happened at the least expected moment. Here I was, just in from playing squash, scruffy as hell, not making any effort, and a total stranger sends me a rose saying that my smile lights up the room! It was just perfect, such a confidence booster.

I watched the man leave with his friends, tall, bearded, not bad looking at all, very presentable.

'It's a shame he didn't ask for your phone number', Deidre said.

'Actually it is not', I replied. 'It's great to have had this moment, it's so exciting, if we had had contact and he didn't live up to expectations it would have spoilt it. Now I have a precious romantic memory. It makes me feel so good. I'll cherish this, as it will probably never happen again.'

'You're right, lucky you! Enjoy your rose! And he was right, you know: your smile often lights up the room, it just took him to recognise it and tell you that.'

I picked up the rose as we left Gino's, most definitely with a smile, a smile that played on my lips for the entire journey home. It was pleasing to feel good about myself again.

Chapter 4

Tango!

We would go to the tea dance at the Garryowen in Hammersmith. If there was a good band on there I would pawn a pair of my shoes and go again at night.

'I've always wanted to learn how to dance the tango', I said to Diane as we met for sundowners on a warm summer's evening in 2003. We had worked together on an HIV and Aids *Know Your Status* campaign, training all our staff and encouraging them to take up the opportunity to get tested. I was Diane's client; she helped us through the process. She was a dynamic entrepreneur with a great sense of humour and we developed a strong and deep friendship.

'Me too, I know the basics of tango but there is a lot of room for improvement', she replied.

'I see Malaysian Airlines are starting direct flights to Buenos Aires from Cape Town, do you fancy coming along? Learning to dance the tango has always been on my list of things to do.'

'Sounds like a plan', Diane said. 'How long would we be away for? I have a lot going on with the business so I can't be away for too long.'

'Just five days. I figure we could do it over the public holiday time, March 21st, that way we don't miss too many days from work.'

'That's good. Once you have more details, let me know and we can make a decision. It sounds like a fabulous break.'

I phoned Diane the next day. It sounded amazing: return flights, three-star accommodation, tickets to dinner and a tango show, and an outing to the pampas to see some gauchos all included in the package at a very reasonable price. We could do some sightseeing ourselves. We didn't need any time to make a decision, it was simple, we were going.

I was pleased that I had something to look forward to around that time. I would be in Buenos Aires for John's birthday, 22nd March 2003; it had been ten years since he had gone away and I was finding this anniversary very unsettling. I had been on my own for ten years now, many of those years fruitlessly searching for him. So many of them were truly wasted years, and at such an important time of my life. Those should have been good years for me, the prime of my life, yet I had wasted them, waiting for John's return. I could never regain that time.

A few days later Diane phoned. 'Do you think we could add another person to the booking?' she asked.

'Who?' I replied. I wasn't someone who enjoyed group outings; even travelling with one other person was difficult for me. I think I had spent just too long on my own and was not the easiest travelling companion for anyone.

'It's Linda, Linda Remke, you know her already through work and at some of my parties. She needs to have a break, she has her young baby now and could do with getting away.'

A few days later I got another call, 'I'm sorry Mary, it's Diane here again. Thanks for organising for Linda, but now there is someone else who wants to join: Yvette, the mother of Mischka, my daughter Monique's friend. She seems very nice, I thought maybe she and Linda could share and then we won't need the triple room.'

'I'll see what I can do.' I put the phone down, muttering to myself. This was becoming a circus. Never mind, no matter what happened I would do what I wanted and if the others wanted to join in or not, that was up to them. We didn't know each other well at all. This could be a recipe for disaster. I resolved to think positive and hope everything would work out for the best.

I told my friend Jenny all about my plans for the trip to Buenos Aires at the Cape Dinner Club a few days later. She and I went to their singles dinner parties once a month but had not met any interesting men there.

We spent most evenings talking to each other, often enjoying our conversation so much better than the stilted conversation we had with many of the men who we encountered there. Jenny was older than I, always beautifully dressed, with short blonde hair and a zest for life that women half her age would envy. Her energy was boundless.

'Did I hear you say that you are going to Buenos Aires?' a guy seated to my left asked.

'Yes, that's right.'

'Lucky you, I learnt Spanish in England recently; it's a lovely language. By the way, my name is Michael.'

'I'm Mary.'

We continued to chat for the rest of the evening; he was English, over in South Africa for a few months' break. Michael was based in Twickenham, separated, and had two grown-up daughters. He was tall, well presented, and easy to talk to. When he asked me out to dinner a few days later I accepted. It was nice to go out with a man for a change. I enjoyed my girlfriends, but it was definitely a different kind of conversation when you were out with a man.

I settled into the routine of going out with Michael very easily. It was a pleasure to be pampered; I hadn't realised how much I still needed to be looked after emotionally. I had survived losing John but although I had rebuilt my life there was a certain vulnerability. I had recovered to an extent but my heart was still fragile. My six year-long search for him had definitely taken its toll.

The night before I left for Buenos Aires Michael invited me out for a going-away dinner. I was late getting to bed, my case wasn't packed, and now here I was needing to leave for the airport in an hour, my bedroom in total chaos, clothes strewn everywhere. What to take, how much room to leave for the shopping I planned to do over there? I didn't even have time to wash my hair. It would all have to wait until I reached Buenos Aires.

I arrived at the airport just in time to be greeted by Diane, Linda, and Yvette. Diane looked at me. 'You seem harassed, are you OK?'

'Yes, I'm fine; I was just running late, which isn't like me, so it threw me out a bit.'

'Never mind, you're here now.'

Before we knew it we were in Buenos Aires. The hotel turned out to be pretty much as expected, small with poky rooms, but clean. There was a drabness about it; thank goodness we weren't planning to spend much time there. The air conditioning didn't work initially but we discovered this was put on by request at the reception. We had a television and put it on to watch the local channel. We were shocked to see that the U.S. had invaded Iraq, and here we were in Buenos Aires, planning to shop up a storm in totally frivolous mode while the world was at war.

We decided to spend our first afternoon wandering around central town, so we would see the Mothers with their white scarves silently protesting and commemorating *los desaparecidos,* those who had disappeared during the old regime. Then we walked to La Recoleta, the cemetery, dark and sombre and very spooky, visiting the mausoleums of the wealthy of Buenos Aires, structures that housed entire families of the dead. As we wandered the narrow alleyways between the greyness of the tombs I felt cold and shivered, goose bumps on my arms despite the warmth of the sunshine. We visited Evita Peron's tomb, as all good tourists should do, but leaving there we needed to do something to shake off the darkness and gloom of La Recoleta and the Mothers clutching photos of their missing children. The only answer was to shop.

We did a whirlwind shop in the leather, shoe, and underwear stores. We left the main shopping area with at least three or four brightly coloured bags each on our arms. Eventually hunger and tiredness got the better of us and we decided to have an early supper before heading back to the hotel.

It had to be steak for dinner; we were in Argentina after all! We found a smart steakhouse and were shown to our table. The room was already quite full. It was old-fashioned, with dark wood panelling and starched linen tablecloths. The noise level was low, people talking in muted voices. Into this haven of gentility the B.A. girls (our new designation from the Buenos Aires trip) arrived, chattering away noisily, giggling and laughingly spreading our bags around us on the floor. We were just so glad to sit down and have a rest from all the walking. Out of nowhere two waiters appeared and even before they handed us any menus they placed chairs behind us, put all our shopping bags on the chairs and then covered them with tablecloths. We had no idea what was going on; here we were, having just visited the cemetery, now sitting at the dinner table with our shopping enshrouded behind us.

It seemed that once this had been done the waiters could relax and get on with the job of taking our order. The meal was superb; Argentina's reputation for great steak was not exaggerated. We decided to go for coffee at the café just around the corner from our hotel. It was a lovely evening and we could sit outside at a pavement table and watch the world go by.

We found a great table, scattered all our bags around us, and then were greeted by a tall, good-looking waiter. His name tag said *Gustavo*. Once again, just like the waiters in the previous restaurant, he seemed agitated when we spread our bags around us. He hurried to find us extra chairs and once again, lifted all the bags onto them, shaking his head and saying it was not good to leave them on the floor. We went along with this ritual for the rest of our time in Argentina, only discovering on our return to South Africa that to leave bags on the floor as a woman signalled you to be "easy"! And here we were, four foreign women—two blondes to boot—scattering our bags merrily on the floor, several of which were emblazoned with the name of an underwear shop, oblivious to the signals we were giving out.

We were having such fun. We spent our days sightseeing, shopping, and having conversations that veered from the totally frivolous to the intensely philosophical. We talked about life, love, and everything else as we walked through La Boca watching the tango displays. There was a vibrancy and brightness about it that was totally captivating: houses with brightly coloured doors and windows were all around us. Diane was interested to learn more about Michael; I had given her some of the detail of how I had met him but she was keen to find out more. She hadn't known me to be involved with anyone since she had met me—except for Juan, of course.

Juan had come into my life in 2000, the year after I had found John, and Diane had been there from the start. I had had a busy day at our Johannesburg offices preparing

Out and about in Buenos Aires

for the testing process of our HIV *Know Your Status* campaign and was not too happy at the thought of a trek to the airport to collect her. I would happily have gone to the hotel and run myself a nice hot bath.

I knew a back way to the airport so I would be able to miss most of the traffic. The journey still seemed to take forever. I glanced periodically in the rear-view mirror. At one traffic light I saw a white Toyota Corolla behind me and could have sworn that the young man in it was smiling at me. *Your mind is playing tricks*, I thought to myself. I decided to pay more attention at the next traffic light. I wasn't imagining anything: not only did he smile, he waved too. *He has a cute face*, I thought as I pulled off. In my distraction I turned one street too early and noticed that the Toyota was still following me. I didn't feel threatened, just curious as to what was going on.

Finally I saw the signs to the airport and yes, the Toyota was still behind me. I took the turn for car rental—this was an Avis car and I would just need to park in their lot briefly while I popped in to the airport to pick up Diane. The man in the Toyota was definitely following me; his car was too old to be a hired car, what was happening here? I straightened my skirt, ran my hands through my hair, apprehensive, but intrigued at what was going on. I got out of the car to find him parked behind me.

He jumped out, moving towards me, a big smile on his face. 'I hope I didn't frighten you, I just wanted to tell you, you are a beautiful woman. I've never done this before, I couldn't help myself.'

I didn't know what to say. He was a good-looking man, younger than I, with an open face and easy smile. What could I say? "Thank you" was as good as it got.

'Are you from Johannesburg?' he asked.

'No, I live in Cape Town.'

'Can I give you my card? If ever you are in Johannesburg again and fancy coffee please call me.'

I took his card and gave him mine. 'Here you are.'

'It was nice to meet you. I'm sorry if I frightened you.'

With that, he got back in his car and drove out of the parking lot. I stood next to my car, a stupid grin on my face, trying to come to grips with what had just happened: being followed to the airport, being told I am a beautiful woman, and all from a good-looking guy several years younger! How bad could that be? I glanced at the card; his firm was based at Midrand, close to our offices. I looked at my watch; I needed to hurry up, Diane was due to arrive at any minute.

'Do you fancy grabbing a quick bite?' I asked Diane, explaining what had happened when I collected her. It felt like being a teenager again, there we were sipping wine, working out an appropriate response to a text message that I had just received from Juan. We both knew it wasn't advisable to meet him in the evening; coffee during the day would be much safer. Diane and I continued chatting over dinner, waiting to hear his reply. Juan confirmed coffee would be good.

I met him the next day at a local coffee shop. There he was, just as I remembered, short brown hair, a golden tan, dressed in jeans and a golf shirt. He stood up and shook my hand, both of us looking embarrassed, and then we started to talk. He had a warm but shy way about him and I felt myself opening up to him.

'Can we meet later for a drink?' he asked.

'Unfortunately I already have an arrangement.'

'Could we meet afterwards?'

'We could, but it would be late.'

'That's OK, we could go for a nightcap.'

'OK, I'll send you an SMS as we are leaving.'

I met Juan at Sandton Square for drinks after my other function. It was a late summer's evening as we sat in the square, telling each other about ourselves, our lives, our hopes and dreams. Many of the tables around us were already empty; waiters scurried around clearing the debris, removing the tablecloths, packing everything away. Eventually we got the message that the bar was closing, we needed to leave. Reluctantly we got up to go.

We said our goodbyes and I left for the hotel, not knowing where to from here. My phone beeped a little later with a thank-you message from Juan, hoping to see me again. I smiled contentedly. *I could do this,* I thought to myself, *he is lovely, and long may it continue.* After that I saw Juan when I travelled to Johannesburg on my monthly business trips.

The relationship was never destined to be serious or to turn into anything long term, but it gave me a boost when I needed it. I had been on my own now for over six years; it was right that I let someone get close to me again. I loved the way Juan smiled appreciatively when he saw me, held my hand as we walked through the streets. There was something about feeling cherished that had been missing from my life for so long. Everything seemed brighter when I was with him, the stars had more sparkle, the colours of the flowers on the sidewalks were more vivid, I could feel the weight starting to lift from my heart, which had been heavy for so long.

The time I had with Juan helped me to rebuild my confidence where men were concerned. I felt attractive and wanted. We could only meet when I was in town, but we continued sporadically until my trips to Johannesburg became fewer and fewer and our relationship died a natural death.

Since Juan I hadn't really been involved with anyone else. It was early days with Michael, I explained to Diane. He was keen, I know. I was enjoying his company but would just have to see how things developed.

Now that the B.A. girls were in Buenos Aires we wanted to learn the tango. Eventually we found a studio where we could have a private lesson. We wanted to avoid the tourist traps, so scouted around for a local studio. Diane, the navigator, got us there safely and we climbed the dingy stairs to the studio. The teacher arrived; he was short with grey, greasy, long hair. We were now becoming exposed to the real roots of the tango, which originated from the sleazy underworld of Buenos Aires.

The lesson went well. I'm not the best dancer, so was barely able to keep up, but at least I grasped the basics. The instructor repeated and repeated the steps until I managed to get the rhythm and keep to the music.

We were due to go to a club where the locals go to dance the tango. We had been told that if we made eye contact with anyone who approached us we had to dance with them if asked. We were apprehensive but agreed to give it a go anyway. We were to be collected by the instructor and taken to the dance hall. The evening started badly when he arrived in a beaten up old car and we lurched precariously down the road. The seats were worn and full of holes, the windows didn't open, the car felt grubby with worn carpets and smelled musty.

We looked at each other. We had wanted to experience the real thing, but was it something we were up to? As we walked into the gloomy, smoky tango dance hall we realised that this was a bridge too far. The raw, sleazy sexuality was overwhelming; the last thing we wanted to do was make eye contact with anyone and have to dance with a stranger. Most of the men looked sinister, with tight black trousers, bright shirts, and gelled hair. The women were provocatively dressed in colourful, revealing outfits that left very little to the imagination. The instructor sat at a table with us. We ordered Cokes and one by one, he took us up to dance. While Diane was dancing with him, Yvette said she was not able to be there a minute longer, this was not where she wanted to be, and so we quickly made our excuses to the instructor and got out of the dance hall as quickly as possible.

We agreed that this was one boundary that would stay firmly in place. We wanted the romantic and sanitised version of the tango; we were not ready for the savage, sleazy tango that was probably its truest form. We had a booked a tango show and dinner as part of the package, and agreed that was going to be more our style. Yes, in many ways it was a copout, but we were obviously not ready to experience the real thing.

The next day we were due to go out to the pampas to see the gauchos. It was good to get out of town. I loved watching the wide-open spaces as I sat quietly gazing out of the window, hardly noticing the chatter of my three companions. I wanted to take some time for myself; I was unused to spending time constantly with other people. I had been on my own for so long.

'You're miles away', Diane said.

'I'm just savouring the moment. Thinking how much has happened in the last ten years.'

'The last ten years?'

'Today is John's fortieth birthday. Ten years ago I was wondering how he was doing on his thirtieth, he had just been gone for a few weeks. I had no idea what was in store for me. So much has happened in the last ten years.'

'What's up?' Linda asked. 'You both look so intense.'

'Just talking about Mary's story', Diane replied. 'It's such an incredible tale.'

They both looked intrigued. 'Tell us more, what is it all about?'

I briefly outlined my story: John and me meeting in London, our "perfect" marriage, then his decision to go backpacking in Australia for three months and his subsequent disappearance, financial ruin, and my long search for him. They were astounded. 'What a story! Who would ever have thought you have had such a time of it? Just look at you now: a good job, a beautiful home, you have so much going for you!'

'I know, I am so blessed to have got through this and come out even stronger. I have decided to write my story. I think it is a story that deserves to be told.'

As I uttered those words I realised I would actually do it. It was a thought that had flitted in and out of my mind, but now putting it into words had made it real. I had committed to write my story, there was no going back.

The trip to Buenos Aires was a pivotal moment in so many ways. The B.A. girls became firm friends and a bond was created of caring and friendship that has helped us through many trials and tribulations. It was also the start of me moving to fulfil my dream of sharing my story with other people, showing that we can overcome what life may throw at us, often emerging stronger and better people for it. I was strong and in control of my destiny now ten years later—would that have been the case if John were still around?

Chapter 5
Travelling Companions

I wasn't better than anyone else but I have always maintained that no one is better than me.

Before I went to Buenos Aires I had already arranged to do a trip to Italy with Peter later in 2003. Peter and I had been friends since 1993; he was half Greek, half Welsh, younger than I, tall and dark. Our last big trip together had been in 1997, when we had gone to track gorillas in Uganda. Another trip was long overdue. Peter and I had a special friendship, easy and undemanding; we understood each other so well. I had met him shortly after John had gone away.

Peter was also keen to try Italy, so we agreed on it as our destination. The next decision was whether to go with a group or to do it on our own. There was no question about that—our experience in Uganda had taught us that we were not suited to group trips, we were both independent and liked to do what we wanted when we wanted. On our trip to Uganda we had had to join a group, as travel to view the gorillas had to be organised through specialised tour operators who were able to obtain the necessary permits. Although we were only eight in the group Peter and I struggled to submit to the constraints of being dictated to in terms of timings, things that we could and couldn't do. We battled over losing our independence in this way. A "footloose" trip, as it was called, would suit us just fine. We could do things at our own pace, stop and start as we wanted to, and just enjoy exploring the Italian countryside together.

The concept was good: eight days walking through a particular part of Italy just carrying a daypack, with water and food for the day and the rest of our luggage transported by the tour operators from lodging to lodging. We decided to do the one called "Umbria and Assisi". It would take us from Todi to Assisi. It was all very exciting and promised to be an adventure. I planned to fly to London first and then to Rome, adding on some time in Ireland afterwards. Peter was flying via Athens on Olympic Airways. I was having quite a year of it—my trip to Buenos Aires in March 2003, and now this in July.

I met Peter in Johannesburg in May; we had done all our bookings and now wanted to firm up some of our plans. There was a further development that he needed to know about. I had met Michael in Cape Town a few months earlier. I would see him before I went to Italy and then he would join me in Ireland afterwards. Peter was noticeably surprised at my news, not unexpectedly as he had never known me to be involved with someone. He was happy for me and wanted to know immediately if I would rather do the Italy trip with Michael rather than him.

'Not at all. We've planned this together; I don't want to do this with anyone but you.'

'OK, if you are sure, but I won't be offended if you would rather go with him.'

'Don't be silly, this is our trip, I've been looking forward to it. I will be spending time with him in Ireland anyway.'

That was settled; I would fly to London, leave some of my luggage at Michael's flat in Twickenham, then join Peter in Rome. A rain jacket was important in case of summer showers and for the rest, good hiking boots and socks and a couple of changes of clothing should do the trick—as well as sunscreen, of course, as it would be the height of summer.

Before I knew where I was, I was standing at Rome Airport waiting for Peter to arrive. Our planes were due to land within an hour of each other, and then we would take the train to Todi.

All went according to plan: as I got into the arrivals hall Peter was there waiting for me, easy to see because he was so much taller than most of the Italians surrounding him. He stood head and shoulders above them.

In Italy

We grinned happily at each other as I pushed my way through the waiting crowds to join Peter and make our way to the train. Our adventure had started.

We had an early breakfast at the hotel—the usual coffee, bread, and jam, not too heavy—and walked to the local deli to buy some water and panini, mortadella, and cheese for the trip. We had some snack bars too; we didn't plan to go hungry, but didn't plan on pigging out either. It was great to be having a healthy holiday, hanging out on the beach wasn't our kind of thing. We had a kitty for all our meals and hoped to come out on our budget. Our plan was to make it a simple trip, no real extravagance. There was no room for this anyway; we were going to be fairly off the beaten track, all small towns barring Assisi, which was to be our last stop.

The first day's hike was going well, just some ominous clouds on the horizon, rain was definitely on the cards and we would see how our rain gear would hold up. According to our route map we were about thirty minutes outside Gianno dell'Umbria when the heavens opened. There was no shelter, nothing for it but to soldier on. The rain was heavy and our raingear, while providing some protection, was not keeping us totally dry.

'Not long now', Peter smiled at me, 'nearly there'. Our rain jackets hadn't been up to the task, both of us were soaked. Our boots were sodden and squelched as we hopped from puddle to puddle.

I smiled back at him. Not the best end to our first day, but it had been fun nonetheless. We approached the hotel; according to our notes it was going to be basic, probably the least comfortable of all the hotels on the route. At this stage, if it was comfortable and dry that was all that mattered. The hotel staff were friendly, concerned at our bedraggled state, hurrying around to get us towels. The room was basic but it had a hot shower and clean towels, which was all we needed. We quickly had our showers, got into some dry clothes, and hung our wet clothes around the room. We went downstairs for dinner; we had to eat in the hotel, as there were no other places around. That was OK; we were tired anyway, just happy to have a quick bowl of pasta and then to bed in preparation for the next day.

Doing the trail was easy. We got into the early-to-bed, early-to-rise routine, eating early in the evening and having just a couple of glasses of wine, as the last thing we wanted to do was to attempt hiking with a hangover.

After the first day we didn't see any more rain—the days were beautiful, sunny and hot. At times we wished for a quick downpour to cool us off. Peter and I chatted when we needed to and fell into a comfortable silence just as easily. We were relaxed as to where we ate, when we stopped, how we would plan our day, as we understood each other very well. We loved the little towns where we stayed—Montefalco, Bevagno, Spello— often bemoaning the fact that after a long day's hike we saw them in the distance generally built on a hill. That last climb was always an effort, but well worth it once we reached the town itself, wandering through the cobbled streets, looking at little shops and restaurants.

We discovered an old-fashioned barber's shop and Peter decided to try out a shave there with a cut-throat razor. All was going well until the barber emerged, eighty if he was a day, his hand trembling furiously. Peter couldn't disguise the look of horror on his face as the aged barber moved towards him, brandishing the razor. We laughed like drains afterwards; what an experience, but not a lot of fun at the time.

We compared the quality of paninis from town to town, picnicking along the route, which sometimes took us along country lanes and sometimes across fields. The lanes were small, just enough space for one vehicle to pass by, often the little bakery delivery van tootling along the road. We passed many roadside shrines with statues and vases full of flowers, and small village churches too. My Italian got us by in the shops and restaurants; it was such a relaxed and easy holiday, we were well tuned in to each other, there was never a moment of friction.

The time came to say goodbye at the airport. We had had a brilliant time, it was all over far too soon. I wished we had been continuing our travels together, it had been too short. But that was the way it was; besides, Michael would be waiting for me back in London for the next wave of my trip.

'See you in South Africa', I said to Peter.

He hugged me. 'Take care, see you soon.' And with that we headed off in different directions.

I think Peter would have liked to be included in my trip to Ireland, but Michael was already on the scene. Glancing at Michael when he met me at the airport, I had a brief moment of doubt as to why I would have agreed for him to join me. We got back to Michael's flat in Twickenham early, which was just as well, as I had to reorganise my case for the trip to Ireland. Kathryn would be there already, and we were going to stay with her at her cottage. I was looking forward to seeing her and my cousins; it was always comforting to be surrounded by family.

I felt a little apprehensive about bringing Michael along. I hadn't intended to do what was beginning to feel like a formal introduction to my family. It was early days in our relationship and a bit too soon to go public. It was too late to think of that now, we were all set to go and I was just going to have to make the best of it and manage people's expectations.

We flew in to Shannon, where we hired a car. Then we drove through to Ballinrobe. I tried to adjust myself to driving on the smaller, winding roads in Ireland; I realised I would need to drive a lot slower than in South Africa, not too many wide, three-lane highways here. We didn't talk much; I kept the radio on for most of the trip, glancing from time to time at Michael, not sure if I was happy to have him here with me. The quietness in the car was not a companionable silence; it felt fractured, as if the space we were in was bristling with static. It wasn't long though before we were at Kathryn's door. She had an old Irish cottage just outside Ballinrobe in Knockgloss; it had a slate roof, whitewashed walls, and myriad colourful plants in the window boxes.

Ballinrobe in County Mayo was the closest place to home I had known, the one constant in my life. Kathryn spent most of the school holidays there at "Katie's cottage". She had spent many years lovingly restoring and furnishing it to make it a truly cosy, old-fashioned Irish cottage.

'Come in; come in', she said, 'you must be shattered after your trip. I'll put the kettle on.'

We brought in our cases and settled down at the dining room table to have tea, coffee, sandwiches, and cake. Kathryn had certainly put on a spread, but then of course that is the Irish way. Her cottage was so very homely, full of familiar things: an old tea set of my parents', my father's old rocking chair.

We had a week there, and were lucky enough to have good weather; we took trips out to the mountains, to Tourmakeady, Ashford Castle, Leenane. We went out for pub meals but also stayed in some nights. I was mindful that having visitors is always expensive so was anxious to ensure that Kathryn wasn't out of pocket. We did some grocery shopping for her now and again. Michael and I had pooled some money to cover these things. Although I knew it was generally expected that the man would pay I valued my independence and did not want to feel beholden to him. We were going to finish off our trip with a barbecue, the weather promised to be good. We popped out to the supermarket to get in some more provisions. Michael got crabby about us buying more supplies for Kathryn.

'But we paid for stuff yesterday', he said.

'Don't underestimate how expensive it is having us stay with her', I replied.

He was not happy with my reply. It wasn't the first time money had been an issue, and it was ringing a warning bell for me. I had always been surrounded by generous people: John had always been like that, my family too, and Peter of course. I was unused to stinginess and felt it denoted a meanness of spirit.

Michael was not relating well to life in Ireland. I knew in my heart I would have been happier visiting without him. I didn't want to make a scene and upset everyone else. I knew I could tolerate the situation to the end of the holiday, be polite and not rock the boat. It wasn't ideal, there was a palpable tension between us, but we managed to stay civil for the balance of the trip. I could see that the family had some questions about what was going on, but they kept their own counsel and left us to it.

I had two days to spend with Michael in London before going back to South Africa. We flew into Heathrow and my heart sank at the thought of getting through the next few days. We barely spoke as the cab took us back to the flat.

Michael had organised National Theatre tickets for us through one of his friends from the pub who worked at the theatre. He had also arranged dinner there on his friend's expense account. We took the train into London from Twickenham; I sat opposite him, looking at him as I would at a stranger. What was I doing there with him, what was I thinking? Since the John experience I had vowed never to compromise on relationships and always be true to myself. If I didn't want to be in a relationship then I had no reason to stay. I was now the most important person in my life.

I decided that the difficult conversation could wait until after the theatre. *Why spoil the evening?* I thought. All I knew was that I wanted to be miles away from there. We arrived at the theatre and were met by Michael's friend. He showed us through to the restaurant and told us to enjoy ourselves. It was lovely; what a treat! The restaurant was full; we sat at a table in the corner. It was very elegant: white linen tablecloths, candles on the tables. I looked at the menu and gulped, the prices were steep.

'Go on, have whatever you want', Michael encouraged me. 'Splash out, after all we are not paying.' He kept encouraging me to work my way through all the courses, adding on coffee and liqueurs for good measure. I couldn't do it. It seemed distasteful to take advantage of someone's generosity, tacky and demeaning. Michael certainly didn't see it that way, and as I watched him tucking in merrily, any feelings that I had left for him vanished.

All in all it was a disastrous evening, the only highlight being the David Mamet play itself. The return train journey was undertaken in stony silence. We sat opposite each other, avoiding each other's gaze. I closed my eyes and pretended to doze, I didn't want to engage with Michael. When we got back to the flat I went straight to bed, berating myself for not confronting the situation. I was tired and fed up; it could wait until morning.

The next morning I joined Michael in the kitchen for coffee. 'That didn't go terribly well did it?' he said. The English are such masters at understatement.

'No', I replied.

'What is your problem?' he said as he turned to face me.

I looked at him. 'What problem?' I replied.

'You know what; you and your entire family are totally dysfunctional, totally abnormal.' He ranted and raved at me for ten minutes, allowing no space for interruptions, at which point I looked him in the eye, left my unfinished toast on the kitchen counter, turned on my heel and went off to pack my case. I did not need to defend either myself or my family to him—my family that had been nothing but kind and hospitable to him.

'And what is with you and Peter anyway? What were you up to in Italy?'

I shook my head at his tirade. I didn't need to justify myself to anyone, I felt no need to engage in a slanging match and continued to pack my case.

'What's the rush?' he said. 'Your flight is only this evening.'

'I don't need to stay here; I have better places to be.'

I continued to pack my case, all the while looking for the card of the minicab firm that had taken us to the airport the week before. I found it at the bottom of my handbag, along with the emerald pendant Michael had given me in Cape Town. I wanted no further part of him. I put the pendant away in his dressing table drawer. It was expensive, I didn't want him to waste money on me, and besides, leaving it behind was a symbolic gesture.

I phoned the minicab firm requesting a taxi. 'What time?' the operator asked. I looked at the time on my cell phone; it was 10:10. '10:30 AM please.'

'No problem, we'll be there at 10:30.' I checked that I had left nothing behind and lugged my case to the door.

'Where are you going?' Michael asked.

'As far away as possible', I replied.

'I can give you a lift to the airport.'

'Don't worry, it is already organised.'

'Let me at least help you down the stairs.'

I allowed him to carry the case down the stairs, as it weighed a ton as usual. I followed behind, taking deep gulps of air, trying to slow my racing heart. This was so difficult but I knew it was the right thing to do.

I was shown out the front door and stood in the garden waiting for the taxi. I glanced at my phone: 10:40 AM, ten minutes late, this wasn't good. I was supposed to be making a dramatic exit, and now here I was waiting like a lemon in the garden, whiling away the time, trying to concentrate on something else, looking at the flowers and neatly clipped hedge but just seeing a blur of colour.

'Come back inside', Michael said, 'it's hot out there'.

My stubborn nature wouldn't let me back down.

'I'm fine thanks; the cab will be here any minute.'

But it wasn't, it was now 11 AM and the taxi was nowhere to be seen. I phoned the office. 'But you booked it for 10:30 AM', they said.

'I know, and it is now 11 AM.'

'No it isn't', they replied, 'it is 10 AM'. Then the penny dropped. My cell phone was on South African time, one hour ahead, that's where I had made the mistake. So much for my grand gesture.

'How quickly can you get here?' I asked sheepishly.

'Ten minutes.'

'That will be helpful, thanks.'

I tried to retain my dignity, holding my head high, standing to attention by the gate, guarding my suitcase. What a relief when the cab finally drew up outside. Michael walked me out and gave me a peck on the cheek. I set off without a backward glance. I arrived at Heathrow, checked in my case, and took a tube back to Knightsbridge to do some shopping. I treated myself to a glass of wine with lunch and tried to make sense of what had happened.

I loved being in Ireland, seeing family and friends, but it had been a mistake going there with Michael. We weren't compatible, and doing the trip there immediately after my trip to Italy with Peter was a big mistake. Maybe it was all too quick. I hadn't taken time to get to know Michael well enough. I had been very hung up on the thought of 2003 being ten years since John had gone away, ten years with no long-term relationship. Maybe subconsciously I felt the need to have someone around. All I do know is that now that I had left him behind I felt as if a weight had been lifted from my shoulders. I was free.

I received a few text messages from Michael when I was back in South Africa, to which I didn't reply; there was no point. What was the use, I was not prepared to open myself up to more verbal abuse. One text message read: *Why is a hill in Italy more appealing than a mountain in Ireland?* I had no answer to that; all I knew was that Peter and I had a long-lasting friendship. We would always be friends; Michael could never ever be in the same league. The trips to Ireland and Italy helped me establish what I did and didn't want; now I could move on. In many ways it was so much easier to have the calmness of a longstanding friendship over the volatility of a romantic relationship. A romantic involvement was great as long as it was with the right person, otherwise it could be a nightmare.

It was a couple of years before I could even entertain the idea of getting involved with anyone again. I had supportive friends and a full social life. Admittedly, a man in my life would add an extra dimension, but he would have to be the right one. I wasn't prepared to settle for second best.

Chapter 6
Finding the Words

During the summer holidays we had not much to amuse us except play down the rocks near the River Robe.

After my brief stay in London in May 2005—when I had done some research for my book, checking out old photos of Cyprus and rediscovering my mother's journal—I developed a romantic notion of spending time on my own in Kathryn's cottage. I knew it would be a good place to be to write and reflect. Being there always gave me a sense of peace and comfort.

'Would it be OK for me to spend a few days on my own in the cottage before you come over for half term?' I asked Kathryn.

'Of course', she said.

I smiled to myself; it was all coming together so well. I was going back to my roots, full circle from my mother's journal, it all seemed so right. I knew I would feel safe there and I would find the strength to face some of the demons I had so carefully ignored for so long. I had left some things out of the book that I had kept to myself. They needed to be included, but I had to find the strength to surface them and confront the bad memories.

There were other reasons for my visit to Ireland. Now that *Remember Me?* was close to being published, I was very aware of people's sensitivities around my portrayal of them. I needed to look carefully at what I had said. I wanted to speak to Nigel in particular, as I was going to reveal a secret he had kept from me for some time and I knew it would not show him in a good light. Nigel had been John's best friend in South Africa; he and John were inseparable. He, like me, had no idea that John's three months away would extend into many years.

I was also secretly intrigued to see Jarlath, the local butcher, again. He had been my very first boyfriend. I had met Jarlath when I was just eighteen years old. We had been over to Ireland on a family holiday.

'Do you want to come to a party?' my cousin Mary Dwyer asked. Kathryn and I had just arrived in Ballinrobe for the summer holidays. It had been a tiring boat and train trip, but I was still up for a party. I had just finished my A Level exams at St. Mary's Convent in Cambridge, and was due to go to university in London in the autumn. I had always been very studious and had not done much socialising. I felt the time had come to let my hair down. I had been sensible for too long. Mary was almost the same age as I, an only child. Whenever Kathryn and I went to Ballinrobe on holidays, we relied on her for our social life.

'Of course', I replied. I definitely wanted to go to a party.

'We'll leave at about ten', Mary said, 'so there's time to freshen up'.

We were staying in my aunt Annie's house in Glebe Street. I loved being with her, she was always so positive, a broad smile on her face, always up for adventure; she had a wicked sense of humour. Kathryn and I unpacked, showered, changed, and then walked down to the flat on Bowgate Street. It was so comfortable being with Annie, my father's younger sister. We had been coming to her house since we were small. Everything was so familiar: the smell of the turf fire in the range; the kettle sitting there, on the boil, ready to make tea at any time; the red light lit in front of the picture of the Sacred Heart. It was home to me, a constant in my life.

It was still light, although it was already late. I loved the long summer evenings in Ireland. It was warm outside, it had been a glorious day. Everything looked so bright and fresh in the soft late evening sun, the flowers in the flowerboxes lining the street were vibrant with colour. We could hear the party before we turned into the street, the sounds of Thin Lizzy coming from the windows. We were welcomed like long-lost friends. Grabbing some food and drink, we began to check out the talent.

The room was quite dark, candles everywhere and the haze of cigarette smoke, which made me sneeze.

As my eyes became accustomed to the dim light they settled on a tall, dark, good-looking man in the corner. He was smartly dressed in a blazer and dark trousers; he looked very sophisticated. He glanced at me, smiled, and then came over to ask me to dance. I smiled back, my face flushed, my heart beating a little faster. I shifted from foot to foot; I wasn't used to flirting.

I liked this man. He was spontaneous and funny, full of joy and laughter. We chatted easily together and he made jokes when I couldn't catch what he was saying, as I was still getting used to his strong accent. His name was Jarlath and he was the local butcher; he lived across the road from Aunt Annie. He asked me out to a dance again the next day and we started to go out regularly. All too soon, though, the summer holiday was over. It was time to go back to Cambridge and start preparations for my first year at university in London.

The next summer I went back, hoping to see Jarlath. He had started going out with someone else, so we couldn't continue our romance. I always wondered how things would have worked out between me and my first love.

Arriving from London almost thirty years later on a warm June morning in 2005 I set off along the narrow, winding lanes. Driving slowly, I had a chance to take in the beauty of the landscape: the fuchsia-filled hedges, the lambs in the fields, the turf drying in the bog. The drive was over quickly and before I knew it I was at Katie's cottage. The cottage was looking lovely: the flowers in the window boxes in full bloom, a fresh coat of paint. It sparkled in the late afternoon sun. The donkey from next door was grazing happily in the adjoining field. It made a perfect picture.

On my first morning there I went to the butcher's. The walk there and the moment of going in the door always affected me in the same way. No matter how many years later it was, my pulse quickened. I fidgeted and played with my hair. I reacted exactly the same as when I was a teenager.

'What can I get you?' the young man behind the counter asked politely.

'Three lamb chops and two chicken breasts, please', I replied, devastated that Jarlath wasn't there. I had taken care with how I looked, hoping to catch a few minutes with him.

After a few days I tried again. This time I found him.

'Hello Jarlath', I said.

'It's lovely to see you', he said. 'You look like a million dollars. How long have you worn your hair like that?'

He smiled at me, a little heavier now, with grey hair, but still the same smile. He passed my parcel of lamb chops over the counter, putting his hand on mine. 'Do you ever think of the old days?'

'Yes, I do.'

'Me too.'

'We had good times, didn't we? How old are you now?'

'Forty-eight. And you?'

'Fifty-three. I was older than you, remember. But I never took advantage of your youth and innocence!'

'No, you didn't, you always behaved like a gentleman.'

'That's right—opportunity lost.'

I smiled at him as I picked up my parcel. Then I turned and walked out into the bright sunshine of Main Street. The thought of what might have been was surely more exciting than anything reality could offer.

I hurried back to the cottage, knowing that I had lots to do. Nigel was due to arrive later that day. I hadn't seen him for many years. He had been such a friend to me in the dark times after John had gone away. We'd had little contact since he'd moved back to Ireland a few years earlier. We exchanged cards at Christmas, and that was about all. To be honest, even in the last few years Nigel spent in Johannesburg I had avoided him. Although we were always friends, just seeing his face reminded me of those difficult days, and times with him were tinged with sadness. Still, I always felt grateful that Nigel had helped me through the toughest times. He had seen me through endless woes during the trauma of not knowing where John was and if he was ever coming home. I knew that he had also felt John's betrayal of their friendship very keenly.

Katie's cottage

There was one particular revelation in my book that did not show Nigel in a good light. It had to be included as it was an essential part of the story, but I was concerned that people might judge him badly. I had made contact with Nigel before my trip to Ireland and was glad that he would come and meet me in Ballinrobe. I wanted to discuss the matter with him face to face. For all those years I had kept the information to myself and now it would become public. I hoped he would understand why I needed to do it.

I busied around the cottage tidying up, preparing a simple meal of chops and potatoes. I felt unsettled, on edge, picking things up and putting them down again, laying and unlaying the table. Nigel phoned me when he was getting close to say that he would be with me in about an hour. I settled down to read my book in the rocking chair in the living room. It had been my father's favourite chair, and as I rocked I felt his calmness surround me. I remembered how he would sit there reading the newspaper from cover to cover, starting off with the sports section. The only sound from him was a rustle of the newspaper when he felt that something unsuitable for his teenage daughters was showing on the television, a signal to my mother to change channels. Kathryn and I always knew where we stood with our father; he provided a peaceful, stable, and nurturing environment that stood us in good stead through the years. His first priority was always the well-being of his family. We were never in doubt as to how much he loved us.

I've never known him to raise his voice to either me or the girls, my mother wrote. *His pint every night and lunchtime was all he asked from life and also his Rugby. He never wanted to reach for the stars or if he did we never knew.*

I was nervous; there was no doubt about it. I closed my eyes and continued to rock, enjoying the silence. Gradually I felt calmer—I was at home here, nothing could faze me.

I glanced at my watch—Nigel would be here soon. I fiddled with the place settings on the table once more and listened for his car coming up the driveway. After what seemed an age, there he was. As I walked out to greet him I noticed that he was looking a little older. His hair had become greyer, he was a little heavier than I remembered, but he was smiling broadly as ever as he came towards me and gave me a big hug. All my worries about raising the subject of the book evaporated immediately. Our friendship was easy and comfortable; it felt as if we had seen each other just the day before.

I had forgotten that I had told Nigel about the possibility of writing my story a few years earlier, so the news about the book wasn't as unexpected as I thought.

'There are things in there that nobody else knows about. Are you OK that I tell everyone about the secret you kept for John?'

He leaned over, held my hand and looked me straight in the eye. 'Of course I am, Mary. Tell the truth. You and I both know why I did it.'

I didn't blame Nigel for keeping the truth from me for so long, but if only I had known that John had left for Australia with another woman I might have moved on so much quicker. Nigel had promised John that he would keep his secret. He, like me, firmly believed that John would be coming back and only many years later did he come clean with me.

'I understand, Nigel. I have never blamed you. I know how loyal you were to John, and how much he disappointed you in the end too.'

'That's fine then. I don't feel I have to justify my actions to anyone. Fire away. I'm looking forward to reading the book.'

He hugged me. The conversation was closed, and we tucked into a hearty meal. Afterwards we left for Ballinrobe to meet Annie. We all walked from her house to one of the pubs on Glebe Street. The houses had been there since my grandparents' time. It was another of those beautiful long summer's evenings, still light and mild. The pavements glistened after the recent rain shower and the sound of Irish music wafted from one of the pubs further down the street. I loved walking through the streets of Ballinrobe; they always stirred up happy childhood memories. Not very much had changed through the years.

Kathryn arrived the next day to perform at the Fleadh Nua, a traditional festival that takes place every year in Ennis Town. She was part of

Kathryn, me and donkey makes three!

a traditional Irish group from London, which played there every year. Nigel and I met Kathryn in Ennis and we had a lovely day together, pottering around the town and visiting a local pub for drinks and a pub lunch. Kathryn chatted easily to Nigel, whom she remembered well from her visits to Johannesburg. She knew what a good friend he had always been to me. It was lovely to spend time with family and old friends—it was so easy. There was nothing to explain, we could just be.

Kathryn and I flew back to London a few days later. She had booked us tickets for a Neil Diamond concert in Earl's Court: a fitting ending to my trip. We got to Earl's Court early to avoid the rush, and the smells of garlic, oregano, and coffee attracted us to an Italian restaurant close by. After a delicious meal of pasta and red wine in the cosy and noisy trattoria we walked the few blocks to the concert. The streets were packed with people heading in the same direction. Many wore Neil Diamond T-shirts; there was a buzz, a feeling of anticipation. Two women brushed past us in a hurry to get to the front of the queue, chatting animatedly and clutching copies of his latest CD. The enormous concert hall filled up quickly as I chatted to the woman sitting in front of me. There was no supporting act billed.

Before we knew it Neil Diamond was onstage. It was a great performance: no support act, no interval, just two hours of energetic performance. I was on the edge of my seat, feeling so much a part of what was happening on the stage. The lighting was superb and added to the atmosphere, people were dancing in the aisles, singing along, clapping furiously. I felt like a teenager again.

I was transported back to the last time Kathryn and I had seen Neil Diamond. It was at the Royal Albert Hall over thirty years previously, when I was just thirteen. I remember walking into the massive arena, with its gilt and red drapes, and looking down from our balcony seats at the full orchestra below me. The lights had dimmed and silence descended on the audience as the sound of African drums came from the depths below. The beat increased as the stage was bathed in candlelight, building to a crescendo as Neil Diamond came on stage to sing "African Trilogy". The beat of the drums vibrated the floorboards beneath my feet. I felt the sound and the rhythm enter my body and soul. I stood up shakily at the end of the show, my whole body tingling. Little did I know then that

Africa was going to become part of my life.

This time was just as good. I was caught up in the music and the lights. So much had changed, but nothing had changed. One day I would grow up—but not just yet.

Chapter 7

Back to My Roots

The bungalow was lovely, bougainvillea and different flowers I hadn't seen before.

Kathryn phoned me not long after my trip to Ireland and England in 2005. 'Don't you fancy coming to Cyprus for Christmas?'

'But you've already arranged to go with Marian', I replied. Our cousin Marian was very close to Kathryn and me; she also lived in London and craved some sunshine for Christmas.

'I know, but she says she wants a separate room, so I will have to pay a single rate. Don't you want to share with me? It'll be cheap; we're only staying for seven days.'

Our last trip to Cyprus in 1989 seemed like a lifetime ago; so much had happened since then. It was hard to believe that the last time I was there I was a happily married woman contemplating many great years ahead with my beloved husband. It was not to be, my life had taken a different path; but on reflection, as I watched the sun slowly setting over the Atlantic Ocean on my veranda in Grotto Bay, I realised how far I had come and how much I had grown through the experiences that I had had. So many years later, and the opportunity to visit Cyprus had come up once again.

'I'll check flights and get back to you', I said, loving the idea. I spent the rest of the evening trawling the Internet and discovered that I could use my British Airways miles to fly to London. I even managed to get onto Kathryn's flight from London to Ercan. It was all falling into place. An added bonus was that I would spend Kathryn's birthday with her: she was a Christmas baby, so Christmas Day was always a double celebration for us.

Peter had family in Cyprus. I told him about my plans to visit the island and he was excited for me, if a little envious! He suggested I look at some property for sale there. It was cheap to buy in Cyprus, he said. *What a lovely idea,* I thought. It would be appropriate to own property in a place associated with such special childhood memories.

Routing via London, I managed to meet up with some family and friends for our usual dinner at the Pink Rupee. London in winter seemed far more Christmassy than in sunny South Africa; I started to get into the festive spirit as I looked at the displays in the shop windows on Oxford Street, their bright lights contrasting with the gloomy darkness of the late winter's afternoon. Rubbing my hands together against the cold, I wished I had remembered my gloves.

It was nice to have a break, as I had been very busy with my book, and had found it stressful reliving difficult moments in the past. I was also starting to get nervous about telling my story, as I had kept so much of it private for so long. Now that I was going public, I needed to be strong. Christmas 2005 promised to be a good one, and hopefully 2006 would see the publication of my book.

We flew with Cyprus Northern Airlines, touching down in Ercan. A hotel bus was there to meet us. It was already dark when we arrived, so I struggled to make out any familiar landmarks but there was something about the smells that reminded me of my childhood. I couldn't put my finger on exactly what it was: probably a mixture of lemons and the sweet heady fragrance of the flowers.

We had chosen to stay at the Acapulco Hotel outside Kyrenia, a stone's throw from the beach where Mother and Fred used to take us as children. The hotel staff were pleasant, greeting us with friendly smiles and showing us to our spacious rooms, with a view of the sea. We unpacked and went downstairs for dinner. We were going to be spoilt for choice during our stay there: the buffet included everything from Indian to Mediterranean to Chinese to bland English fare. Luckily the hotel had a gym, a heated indoor pool, a Turkish bath, and a spa, so we would have ample opportunity to work off all that food! Just as well, I thought to myself, as I was in training for the Knysna half marathon. Since John had gone away I had done so many things I would probably never have done if he had been around: a game ranger course, scuba diving, and now, at this late stage in my life, running. In many ways his leaving me had liberated me from being just a wife to being a person in my own right. There was no question that I had reinvented myself in the last few years.

Yes, I had definitely moved on, I thought, as Kathryn, Marian, and I left the hotel the next day in our hired car and set off for Kyrenia, our "home" town. Marian had been a good friend to us both through the year. She was a few years older than we, the eldest in my mother's sister Marie's family. She had a strong sense of family and was often instrumental in arranging times when we all got together. We were experiencing Kyrenia in 2005, over fifty years since the time my mother spoke about in her journal. It was a magical place loved by our parents too:

They took us to the beach to Kyrenia. Kyrenia is my favourite place in all the places I've been there is no place quite like it.

Kyrenia represented a coming home for me, just as Ballinrobe did. We parked on the outskirts and, ambling into the town, were delighted to find that little had changed since our childhood: the streets couldn't be widened so were still narrow and steep with cobblestones, and the sailing boats bobbed around in the harbour as they had always done. It was comforting to recognise so many familiar things after all this time—even the Dome Hotel and the little harbour cafés were still there.

Reacquainted with Kyrenia, we set about exploring the countryside and the many Crusader castles perched on the hills. Fortunately it was winter, so we managed the steep walks up to their parapets, probably not such an easy feat in the summer months. It was amazing to look out from the ramparts over the sea to Turkey in the same spot where Richard the Lionheart would have stood in the time of the Crusades. We huffed and puffed our way up the broken steps and, perching on the lookout towers, gazed at the familiar fields beneath us. Memories of my happy childhood filled my mind and heart.

The island was still largely unspoilt in the north; the Turkish part had not seen the massive development that had taken place in the Greek south. Now it appeared that that was about to change. Many billboards were going up advertising hotels and apartments for sale, and at very reasonable prices. The thought of buying something here was more and more tempting. I couldn't do it on my own though—it would just be too much of a stretch. Peter had been interested, but being of Greek descent, buying in the north wouldn't work for him. I put my thoughts on back burner; I needed to be realistic, after all. Still, it seemed a shame to miss the opportunity, as it would have been so meaningful to have a solid connection to Cyprus again. It had been such a pivotal part of my childhood; it was here that I had come to appreciate different cultures, different ways of living, the heat and wide open spaces.

The next day we took a back route from Kyrenia further east towards Kantara Castle, negotiating hairpin bends on the tiny winding road. I clutched the steering wheel, slowing down considerably. I wasn't used to such narrow roads and the bends were definitely keeping me alert. As we drove further and further out, the road became narrower, with the sheer drop to the sea becoming markedly more precarious. The chatter in the car stilled. None of us spoke, we all looked ahead, willing the little car to cling to the road, praying that we wouldn't encounter another car coming in the opposite direction.

The castle was worth the drive, and once we were there we relaxed

Kantara Castle

The view at Kantara

again, all trying to speak at once, interrupting each other, a noisy family outing. On our way back we saw a small development of just twenty-odd houses, a little way out of town with a view of the sea and the Kyrenia Mountains. We slowed down and I asked Kathryn to take a photo of the board and some of the surrounding area, ostensibly to give details to Peter. I didn't want to talk to her too much yet about my scheme of buying here. I didn't feel ready to put it into words—I was still thinking it through, and perhaps it *was* just pie in the sky.

That night in our room I broached the subject with Kathryn. The houses weren't expensive—what did she think of going in half with me, sourcing a bond in England, as the interest rates would be far more favourable than those in South Africa? We agreed that I would contact the developers the next day and do a site visit. The agent agreed to meet me at the Pia Bella Hotel in Kyrenia and I left Kathryn and Marian there having tea in the elegant surroundings while I went to inspect the site.

I loved what I saw. It was a small development of two- and three-bedroomed villas, each with a garden and space for a private pool. I liked the fact that it was out of town and within walking distance of a beach. I loved the olive trees in the field next door, the view of the mountains and the sea. It still felt rural, a discreet development.

Kathryn and I talked at length about the ramifications of buying in Northern Cyprus, particularly in the light of Cypriot land disputes with the Greeks of Southern Cyprus. But we resolved to pursue things. We would gather more information and then make an informed decision as to whether we should go ahead.

After much deliberation we agreed that we should take the risk and signed for No. 3 Tatlisu (Sweet Water) Village. We had fun over the next months, watching our dream slowly translate into reality. It brought back many memories of the trials and tribulations of building at Grotto Bay when I was still based in Johannesburg. But I knew it would be worth it in the end. In the following months as the house was being built, Kathryn and I worked together with the builders to ensure that things were progressing well. Electricity was a problem, as the mains supply wasn't on yet. That would come in due course. In the meantime we had only a contractor's low-voltage electricity connection. We also had to get our water tank filled before the plumbing was connected to the mains water supply. To arrange this we had to visit the mayor in Tatlisu on our next trip the following year, when we went back to put the finishing touches to the house.

After driving up the winding road to the village, past the olive groves and the goats grazing in the fields, we were ushered into a room in the council building by a man wearing the traditional Turkish black baggy pants. We had to see the mayor personally to request our water supply, as his approval was essential. The office was in a building centuries old. We sat patiently on the wooden benches outside until the mayor was prepared to grant us some time. The smell of strong Turkish coffee came down the corridor. I walked around the office, glancing out of the window at the olive and lemon trees in the dusty fields. The dry brown earth was in stark contrast to the dark shiny leaves and the intense blue of the sky. While we were there we checked for mail for ourselves and our neighbours. This involved going into another room where a large drawer was opened, each compartment within it holding mail for different areas. I loved the slow order of things here. Why should things go at breakneck speed? Everything would happen in its own good time, as it had been doing for years.

Furnishing the villa at a distance was a challenge. Fortunately there were people who specialised in sourcing furniture, so Kathryn and I checked colour schemes and finishes over the Internet. It was remarkable how similar our tastes were: we agreed on the colours, the style of furniture; it was all so very easy even though were living continents apart.

It was great to have some roots there, as Cyprus always held happy memories for me of my childhood in the sun and it was wonderful to share it with Kathryn and create a home together. It somehow felt appropriate that Cyprus had been the catalyst for the rekindling of our relationship, as the island had in many ways made me who I am. So many years had passed since Elsa Fisher had pointed out to us the importance of family, and here we were all those years later, recreating our childhood bond.

Cyprus - Tatlisu Villa

Chapter 8
A Published Author!

No hiding anymore.

Returning from my trip to Cyprus I needed to focus on my book again—I was determined to have it published in 2006. After a couple of months it was ready. I had done my final edits and I needed to submit it to a publisher for review. Patience has never been one of my virtues, and I could barely stand the wait to hear if the manuscript had been accepted. I was full of self-doubt: would they hate it? What if they thought it was boring, inconsequential? It was a big story for me but would it be a big story for them? The publishers had said three months and they took every day of that, only to give me my dreaded first rejection!

My book didn't fall into any of the categories that South African publishers were supporting, so I decided to self-publish. I had been through the painful process of writing my story and now I was determined to get it out there, even if it was just for a small audience. My friends had always been supportive, encouraging me with presents of pens and journals to write in. I couldn't let them down. My book would be published, come what may.

At last the book was edited and designed—all that remained was for it to go to print. I had decided from the outset that the cover image would be a painting of my house at Grotto Bay by a local artist, Osnat. The effect was bright and busy—not what a professional publishing house would have gone for—but it was just what I wanted.

It is hard to describe the excitement of getting the book back from the printers. I could hardly believe that I had done what I had set out to do: write a book and publish it. I slept with it under my pillow the first night. I spent a short time listening to the rhythm of the waves before turning over and going into a deep and contented sleep. It was done. It was such a thrilling thought that I had been responsible for it from start to finish— it was mine, warts and all.

I decided to hold launch parties in Johannesburg and Cape Town, as I had groups of friends in both places. The launches were as much celebrations as they were PR opportunities. *Remember Me?* was a very personal memoir, and as so many of my friends had been on the journey with me, I wanted to acknowledge and celebrate with them.

'Best of luck for tonight', my friend Nicky said over the phone. 'I'm sure it will go well.' I had met Nicky when I first visited Grotto Bay in 1994 looking for a plot. She was the estate agent there, a short, bright, bubbly lady. She helped me through the process of building my house and became a good friend. We spent many evenings together, chatting on the veranda in Grotto Bay, watching the sun set over the sea as Nicky saw me through the rebuilding of my life. She was always there to offer support when I needed it; I didn't need to ask, she somehow sensed it. She knew how hard I had worked to finish my book, what a momentous and emotional occasion launching it would be for me, and the memories it would surface.

Nicky had told me that she would not be able to join me for the first launch in Johannesburg, but would travel from Grotto Bay to be at the Cape Town launch a few weeks later. I was glad the first launch was going to be in Johannesburg, it seemed appropriate somehow. My book reflected the struggle I had gone through to survive after John's disappearance. So much of that period was spent in Johannesburg, and so many of my friends were still based there and would be coming to the launch.

'Thanks Nicky', I replied. 'Fingers crossed. Everything is arranged. Let's just hope everyone shows up.'

'I'm sure they will. They'll all be dying to read your book.'

I put the phone down and continued putting the final touches to my make-up. I was using a bit more than usual. I wanted to look my best. I knew I was going to see friends I hadn't seen for years. The last thing I wanted was for them to think how much I had aged. I turned the air conditioning on in my hotel room at the Palazzo Montecasino. It was spring in Johannesburg but a particularly warm day and I didn't want to arrive at the launch all hot and bothered. I knew it was an extravagance to spend the night there, but it meant just a short walk downstairs to the Irish pub, Cobblestones, instead of having to make my way through Johannesburg's afternoon traffic.

Almost ready to go. I checked my reflection in the mirror and liked what I saw. Then I glanced quickly at my notes. I knew I had to make a speech but I didn't want it to be rehearsed; something spontaneous and from the heart was far more me.

I took a deep breath, fingering the gold locket my parents had given me for my eighteenth birthday. I knew how proud they would have been and I was glad that in some small way they would be with me for this occasion. I drew such strength from them and the strong faith they had given me. In the difficult days after John left I had turned more and more to the Church, attending Mass regularly, lighting candles and praying for John's safe return and the ability to get through the hard times. I had always been a regular churchgoer, but now there was an intensity about my prayer when I lit my candles. I closed my eyes tightly, willing my prayers to be answered, and slowly calmness would descend and my body would relax. It would come right, it just had to.

Time to go. I walked down the stairs through the lobby and out into the sunshine of the spring evening. I made my way towards Cobblestones. I was excited but also very emotional. I had opened myself up so much in the book, and now everyone was going to hear my story. What were my friends going to think? I hadn't told them everything, wanting to retain a certain amount of privacy. Would they be cross? Would they resent the fact that I had held some information back from them? Only time would tell. It was all out there now, too late to take it back.

At least my family had reacted positively, despite the additional revelations. I had sent my sister, Kathryn, the book with strict instructions to read it before letting the rest of the family see it. She was saddened by the details of the hardships I had hidden from my family and friends, not wanting to worry them. She said how difficult it was to realise all these years later just how tough things had been for me. But she liked the book and had nothing bad to say. What a relief—I had been on tenterhooks until I got her feedback. Perhaps I should have opened myself up more to my friends and family at the time, I thought to myself, but at the end of the day that was my decision and I would have to bear the consequences.

I walked through the Montecasino complex, and finally arrived at Cobblestones. I had chosen the pub for the launch as it had an intimate and welcoming feel to it: soft lighting, lots of cosy corners. I didn't want a stuffy, formal affair—the launch was to be more of a party, a chance to celebrate the new Mary with my friends.

How appropriate that Des Lee was going to play for us! John and I had often gone to hear him in the early '80s when we were newly arrived in Johannesburg. He had played in Ireland with the Miami Showband and had now made South Africa his home. He was going to play some Irish songs for me—just what I wanted, and in a familiar Irish-style pub environment.

I went over to the table set up for the book signing and checked the boxes of books. I had no idea how many I would need. Would people want to buy them? I started to feel niggles of doubt. What if no one wanted them? It didn't matter, I thought to myself. I wrote my book because I had to do it. If people didn't like it, so be it.

Just as I looked up from counting the books, Deirdre arrived with her sister Manda in tow. They looked so alike, dressed in vibrant colours, with broad, infectious smiles. Deirdre was the first person I confided in after I found John, six years after he left. She had come to my office and spent time with me as I tried to calm down after speaking to him.

'Here we are, ready for duty', said Deirdre, putting a petty cash tin on the table and starting to build a display of books. As soon as that was done she got to work putting up my posters, showing the cover of the book, in strategic areas. There could be no doubt that this was the venue for my book launch. The bold cover of *Remember Me?* by Mary Monaghan was there for all to see.

Finally everything was ready. It had been such fun preparing the invitations, tracing people from my old days at American Express and Nedbank. As I had been working there when John left, many of my colleagues had known him and had been part of my search for him. I was glad that they could now be part of my new beginnings. They had seen me struggle to come to terms with the realisation that John wasn't coming back and had watched me slowly rebuilding my life.

Slowly my guests started to arrive. It was touching to see so many good friends who had stood by me through those awful times: Moira, Pam, Archie—oh, and there's John Raath, whom we had only managed to make contact with that very morning! Joan was talking to some figures from the past, Phil May and Brendan Ambrose, old stalwarts of the Irish Club in Hillbrow.

I became trapped behind the table, frantically signing books. Some people were buying two or three for friends and family. I strained to find a gap between the people standing in front of me as I tried to see who had arrived.

The place was humming, people renewing acquaintances with old friends they hadn't seen for years. Des Lee was playing "Fields of Athenry" in the background, snacks were circulating, drinks were flowing. My nerves started to subside; I was surrounded by friends who would understand and appreciate my book. It was going to be OK. It felt like old times, so many people from the old days, chatting and drinking together, Irish music playing. The only one missing was John.

I greeted Diane, a relatively new friend in comparison to most of the people there. She had been with me at the start of my writing journey when, on our trip to Buenos Aires, I first declared my intention to write a book. She had encouraged me all along the way and had agreed to give the speech introducing me. I asked her to keep it simple and not too emotional. I was so close to tears—tears of pride and happiness that I had got here, but also tears of sorrow as I remembered what I had gone through. Looking at all those faces from my past reminded me of the days when life was so dark for me.

I smiled up at Lynn, who was there with her daughter Samantha. I had known them since I had first arrived in Johannesburg in 1981. They were such good friends, always there for me. I signed their books with a flourish. It was hard to express in words the debt of gratitude I owed to so many people.

'Diane is waving at you', Deirdre said. 'I think it's time for the speeches.'

It was indeed.

Here goes, I thought to myself. I muttered a quick prayer and joined Diane near the stage. Des Lee finished his song and introduced Diane.

'In 2003 I went to Buenos Aires with Mary and two other friends, Yvette and Linda', Diane began. 'We were there for a trip of sightseeing, shopping, and tango lessons. We had become friends through a business relationship not long before that. It was on that trip that Mary told us she planned to write a book about her life story. One thing about Mary is that if she puts her mind to something that is exactly what she does … '

I listened intently as Diane spoke a little about my long writing journey before she passed the microphone to me.

'Thank you so much for coming', I said. 'It is hard to describe how much it means to me. Many of you here today were part of my story and helped me through some very difficult times. Thank you so much for always being there for me.

'Writing my story has been an adventure, and has meant revisiting many old hurts. But all along I believed it was a book that had to be written—not only for myself and my friends, but as a source of inspiration to others. I survived, you can survive, times can be tough but you can get through and that is what I want this book to be seen as: a story of survival and new beginnings.

'I can now avoid having to recount my story to people at parties who meet me and ask, "Are you married? Oh dear, and what happened then?" Now I can simply tell them to read my book.

'I hope you enjoy the story and I hope you will always remember me as I remember you.'

I felt tears welling up in my eyes as I listened to the applause of my friends. I had done it—I had written my book and it was going to be read by all these people. It was a scary thought, but there was no turning back.

Diane grabbed my arm. 'This book is going to change your life', she said.

'Yes, let's see what it brings', I replied.

'Here's a glass of wine.'

'Thanks, it's the first one of the evening; I

Johannesburg book launch

thought if I had something to drink before the speeches I might become even more emotional.'

'Cheers', she said as we clinked glasses. 'I am so proud of you.'

'Thanks; I know I shouldn't say it, but I'm proud of me too! Let's party now!'

A week later, I held the Cape Town launch at Kennedy's in Long Street. Again, I had an Irish band with Maurice Judge, who had been part of the Irish music scene in Johannesburg for many years. It was good to see so many friends here too: mostly ex-work colleagues, business associates, friends from Grotto Bay, and members of the Women's Writing Workshops I had attended over the years.

I had gone to the Women's Writing Workshops shortly after my decision to write a book, attending several courses specifically aimed at women who were interested in writing their stories. Now, at Kennedy's, I was again in a relaxed, party-like environment, celebrating life and bursting with pleasure: pleasure in the love of friends, pleasure in my achievement. This was something I had done by myself, for myself. I had truly become my own person.

My writing buddy, Bridgett, gave the speech and once again we had a great evening. She had lived in Canada for most of her childhood, returning to South Africa after 1994, the year of the first democratic elections. Bridgett had watched me grapple with what to include and had been an excellent sounding board, always full of encouragement. I was surrounded by Cape Town friends, many of whom had been an integral part of my writing process and had watched my book develop over time. I knew that they appreciated what it had taken to get to the final version of *Remember Me?* Diane was there too, back home in Cape Town after her business trip to Johannesburg. She took me aside. 'I meant what I said in Johannesburg', she said. 'This will change your life, just you wait and see.'

After the launch I waited anxiously for reaction to my book, feeling terribly exposed. Now that my story was aired in public, I felt a lot lighter; it had probably been misguided to keep so much of it to myself. I had always been a very private person, never discussing the natural ups and downs of my marriage with anyone else. Now here I was, baring it all in the public arena, but it felt right. I knew my story had to be told, and I hoped that in some way it would help people in similar situations. That was the theory, anyway.

But what if people hated my book, thinking I was ridiculous for holding on to my marriage for so long, searching for John and still, in some way, loving him? I moved on when I was ready to do so. Yes, to some it may have seemed far too long, and they might think I was a fool for not seeing the writing on the wall; but it was what I needed to do. I had to give John the benefit of the doubt until I accepted the truth and found myself ready to start afresh and put him behind me.

Within a day reactions started to come in, all of them supportive. Many of my friends from the old days felt bad that they hadn't been as helpful as they might have been had they known the full extent of my troubles. I hadn't told anyone about my dire financial straits, for instance. I was too proud to let anyone know that I'd had barely enough money for food. They would gladly have helped me, I know, but somehow I had wanted to battle through on my own.

I breathed a sigh of relief as good wishes filled my email inbox. My family and friends liked the book—that was all that mattered. My cousins and my aunt Annie in Ireland were full of praise, and sad to follow the story of my trials and tribulations. Annie had been such an integral part of my life, and was so proud to be mentioned in the book.

I had told the story of her checking my Claddagh ring after my annulment. There is a particular way of wearing this ring, which is from the west of Ireland. The ring shows a heart held by two hands, with a crown on top. If the heart is worn so that it shows itself as open, it means that you are available; should it be closed you are taken. When I visited Annie shortly after the annulment she checked my ring to see that I was showing myself as "open". I had been worried about her acceptance of my annulment, feeling insecure about how she would view my turning my back on my marriage, but this moment indicated that she was accepting of what I had done and supportive of my need to start afresh. She didn't remember it, but to me it was a moment of major significance: she had given me her blessing to move on. It made me realise how often the small things we do for other people are forgotten or their significance not understood. It had been a small thing to her but a turning point for me.

I had printed enough books to stock book stores as well; it now remained to be seen if my book could reach a wider audience. Yvette and

Dorria from Redhedz helped handle the PR. They contacted TV, radio, and print media to see if any of them were interested in running a piece on my book. The first reaction was from SABC TV's *Morning Live* programme, asking me to appear on the breakfast TV show in two days' time. That was a good start, I thought to myself. The studios were on Beach Road in Sea Point, where I jogged every morning. At least it would be familiar territory.

Now what to wear? I decided on something comfortable so that I wouldn't feel ill at ease. I would be nervous enough without having to worry about my clothes. I had to be at the studio at 6:15 AM—no problem for me, as I have always been an early riser. I was up at the crack of dawn, carefully putting on the clothes I had laid out on a chair the night before. I didn't want anything to rattle me—I wanted to be calm and ready for this. After making some coffee I sat quietly on the couch, willing myself to do the best I could. I needed to still myself, to feel centred.

I said a quick prayer that all would go well. As I sat there my breathing slowed, my body relaxed, the chatter in my head subsided. Through all the stressful times after John had disappeared I found comfort in my Catholic faith, it grounded me and kept me calm no matter how difficult things became. The familiarity of lighting candles and reciting my prayers gave me strength to carry on. At that time of the day there was hardly any traffic, so I got to Sea Point well ahead of time. Parking the car close to the promenade, I watched the waves on the rocks and the boats on the horizon.

I walked over to the studio and was shown to the waiting area. I wasn't sure what they would do about make-up, but it was all very casual and no further preparation was required. They would simply cross from the studio in Johannesburg to me in Cape Town. They gave me an earpiece, pointed me at the camera and the next thing I knew I was live on TV. Vuyo Mbuli interviewed me. After my initial discomfort at looking straight into the camera lens I relaxed, realising that I wouldn't see who I was talking to. The questions were interesting and the time flew by. Relieved when it was over, I started walking back to my car. I hadn't got very far when the phone started ringing. My friends had all been watching and thought I had done well. It felt strange to get back to the car park. It seemed like a lifetime ago that I had sat gazing at the waves before going into the studio. I had now put my story out there; it was in black and white for all to see.

After the show, requests for radio interviews started to come in. One of the first was from Lynn Baker, at CCFM in Muizenberg. She had read the book and had many searching questions for me. I was also on Lisa Chait's Cape Talk show, where listeners phoned in with questions: *Why did it take you so long to move on? Have you heard from John since?* It was strange fielding calls about my relationship with complete strangers, but I knew that I had laid myself open to it. What was most difficult was that, while I had been prepared to answer questions about the period dealt with in the book, I hadn't anticipated being asked about my life now. That caught me off guard. I hadn't spent the time analysing where I was now, in contrast to the constant review and analysis of the period of John's disappearance.

As sales of the book started to take off I planned a trip to Johannesburg to do interviews with SAfm, the national radio station, and Kate Turkington on Radio 702 for her show, *Believe It or Not*. I felt confident now talking about my story. I had received many emails of encouragement from readers and listeners, telling similar stories and praising me for my honesty and lack of bitterness towards John. It felt good. I was simply expressing what I felt. Some people might say I had been weak and gullible waiting for him for so long, but I knew at the time it was the right thing to do. Surprisingly, many of the supportive responses were from men, almost apologising on behalf of men for what had happened to me. It was incredible, not one nasty response. I had not expected people to write to me and was very touched that my story had reached them.

Your talk was both sad and inspiring.
I thought it fitting to let you know that your positive response to hardship and your resolve to not be embittered was truly inspirational.
Your interview on Kate Turkington's show was riveting and needless to say for many ... thought & emotion provoking.

I was humbled. I had written *Remember Me?* from the heart, and I think that is what people appreciated. I didn't pretend to be anyone other than who I was. I felt in my heart I could forgive John, and I just wanted my story to be told. I suppose I knew that I probably wrote it in some way for him, to tell him what life had been like for me. The sad thing was that he would probably never get to read it.

Chapter 9
Bringing It All Home

Uncle Martin used to tell us about New York and when he went it took him six weeks to get there.

It was February 2007 and several months since my book launches in South Africa. I had been busy with interviews here and there. I had even managed to fit in a trip to Cyprus at Christmas to put the final touches on furnishing the house with Kathryn. It had been a good project and had given us precious opportunities to spend time together. Between building the house in Cyprus and my book, our relationship had matured into something far deeper than it had ever been. We were not sisters who shared our personal lives easily and there were many things still probably left unsaid, but our connection had become very strong.

'Liam says you should phone him if you get a chance. He's sure he can do something to help you market the book in Ireland', Kathryn said.

We had known Liam for many years; he was a freelance journalist working from Ballinrobe, younger than we, a keen sportsman. Kathryn had got to know him well when he was working to promote Ireland's Lake District as a tourist destination. Kathryn helped him as much as she could with contacts and administration in London.

Two days later I gave him a call.

'I can put together an article focusing on the Ballinrobe connection for you, but you need to have some form of distribution worked out',

Liam said. 'It's pointless telling people about the book if they can't get their hands on a copy.'

'You're right. I'll work on that and once I've got something set up I'll let you know.'

It all seemed so simple. I'd contact some book distribution companies in Ireland and see what I could organise. If only it were that straight-forward! Day after day I fired off emails, to be met with no response or a standard negative response. The same held true for printers over there. No one seemed interested in taking on my book.

I decided to put my efforts on hold until after my trip to New York in March 2007. It was to be the first wave of my fiftieth birthday celebrations. Kathryn had treated me to a stay there and had arranged a hotel booking for us. All I had to do was get to New York. At the very last minute she told me that our cousin Mary Dwyer was going to be there too.

I arrived on a chilly, grey, spring morning. It had been a long flight from Johannesburg and I was feeling quite jaded. I picked up my bright yellow suitcase, always easily identifiable on the baggage carousel, and walked out into the arrivals hall. It was packed with people of all nationalities, shapes, and sizes.

I had booked a shuttle to the hotel, as the cost was very reasonable and it meant that Kathryn didn't have to get up at the crack of dawn to meet me. I located a telephone and rang the Super Shuttle number. 'Your shuttle will be there in fifteen minutes, ma'am. Please stay in our designated waiting area.' *Not so bad*, I thought, as I wheeled my trolley over and joined all the other bleary-eyed, jetlagged passengers. They sat on the benches, some dressed in warm clothes, some in summer clothes, all equally tired, one of them tapping his feet incessantly, impatient to get the last segment of his trip over with. Fifteen minutes came and went and it was well over forty-five minutes by the time the shuttle came. It was a relief to see it approaching. Climbing aboard, I grabbed a seat at the back, put my head against the window and prepared for my first impressions of New York.

It was a Sunday morning, but the traffic was still heavy. Exhausted as I was, I eagerly took in the famous cityscape which until now I had only experienced on TV or in the cinema. It was just as I imagined it: as we sped along the roads I could feel the energy, the fast pace. All those familiar buildings were now to be seen for real. I had seen them so often before on the big screen and now I was experiencing them first-hand.

I listened to the excited chatter of the other people in the shuttle, some returning home from holidays, some tourists like me. We were a wide mix of nationalities: Indian, Mexican, Thai, African, Irish, English. The Big Apple was certainly cosmopolitan. We found a common language, gasping in unison as the driver swerved and braked, weaving in and out of the traffic. Welcome to the New York way of driving!

Not a minute too soon, I breathed a sigh of relief as we arrived safely at the Broadway Plaza Hotel. I took the small lift up to the room and Kathryn opened the door with a broad grin. 'You made good time! Why don't you freshen up while I grab us some breakfast from the breakfast room? I can hardly wait to catch up with all the news.'

I looked at our hotel room. It was just as small as I'd expected, but we only needed to sleep there, after all. The bathroom, on the other hand, was enormous—totally disproportionate to the size of the bedroom. I had a quick shower and changed. Feeling much better, I went back into the bedroom to enjoy my first New York breakfast: bagels, cream cheese, and coffee. I was determined to do everything the American way. The coffee smelt rich and strong, just what I needed to get over my jetlag. I tucked into the bagel, savouring every calorie-laden mouthful. I felt like a true New Yorker.

Kathryn glanced at her watch. 'I think it's best for you to just keep going and adjust to the new time zone. That's the only way to get over the jetlag. From tomorrow we can do whatever you want to, but for today I'm taking charge.' Kathryn's tone brooked no argument; despite my freshening up I still felt weary, so was happy to go with the flow.

'OK, as long as your programme involves some walking. I want to stretch my legs after the long flight.'

'Of course it does, put on some comfortable shoes, and then we'll set off. We'll start with Grand Central Station, and then we'll go on to the Metropolitan Museum and Central Park. I'll just send Mary a text message to say that you've arrived safely. She is staying with her son David. We'll probably meet up with her for dinner tonight.'

I grabbed my jacket; I was definitely feeling the temperature difference between Cape Town and New York.

'Let's go', said Kathryn with an air of authority. She certainly meant business. We arrived at Grand Central Station and walked towards the clock in the centre of the concourse. 'Look up at the ceiling', she said, 'the frescoes are amazing'. I moved to get some space, trying to get out of the way of commuters running to catch their trains. It was a busy station but its high ceilings gave it a lightness and feeling of expanse. I obediently looked up. 'Turn a little to the left; you'll get the best view from that angle.' The frescoes were indeed amazing. I loved the sparkling stars, so unexpectedly pretty in this setting.

As I gazed up at them I felt a tap on my shoulder. 'Well, how'ya?' It was my aunt Annie from Ballinrobe, grinning from ear to ear. My cousin Mary was with her.

'My goodness, what a surprise!' I said. 'I had no idea you were coming. I can't believe you have finally made it over here, good for you!' I knew Annie had never done more than a three-hour plane trip, so a trip to New York was a big deal for her.

Kathryn smiled. 'You see, I can keep a secret. Thank goodness we've done it. It has been such a strain setting it all up!'

Mary was a regular visitor to New York and knew all the best spots. It was Annie's first time there. She had come to surprise me, and what a lovely surprise it was! She had a mischievous sense of humour and our times together were always full of laughter. Annie's energy was endless, belying her age. For a long time I had tried to persuade her to visit South Africa, but she always refused. 'I'll come when I need to buy the hat', she would say. This was her way of letting me know that she would come in the unlikely event that I were to get married again, so the chances were slim that she would ever visit me in Africa! We chatted away over coffee and agreed to meet up later that night for dinner. My trip had turned out to be a real family get-together.

My time in New York was going to be very short, but there were some things I absolutely had to do. I'd already ticked off the Metropolitan Museum and the frescoes on the ceiling of Grand Central station—now I had to visit Ellis Island. It was a place of significance to anyone Irish, as it was the first point of entry for the boats carrying Irish immigrants to the United States. Many of our relatives would have arrived there with the hope of a brighter future, leaving behind Ireland's famine and poverty.

Kathryn and I got up early the next morning to make the trip to Battery Park, where we would catch the ferry. The weather forecast the night before had promised a nice and sunny day—twenty degrees. We dressed accordingly, quite lightly, but with jackets to counteract the stiff breeze from the water. As we arrived at Battery Park, Kathryn and I

On the ferry to Ellis Island

looked at the sky with apprehension. It had turned grey and misty, and the air was suddenly bitterly cold. No sign of the sunshine we had been promised. We were dressed totally inappropriately, but decided to carry on anyway.

After paying our money at the ticket office, we boarded the ferry, determined to stay on deck to get the best views. With a loud blast of the horn, the boat set off. We watched as the Statue of Liberty came closer— it appeared and disappeared from view as the mist swirled around it, the torch showing intermittently through the fog. My hands were turning blue with the cold and my nose had turned to ice. I was shivering, uncomfortably cold as we approached Ellis Island. In some ways I wasn't sure if I was shivering from the cold or shivering at the thought of what Ellis Island represented for the Irish and so many other immigrant groups as they abandoned their harsh existence in their own countries in search of a better future. So many of my countrymen had made this journey on coffin ships, so called because of the high death rate of those who sailed on them as they fled the Famine in Ireland.

'Not long now', Kathryn said, encouraging me to hang on. As Ellis Island came into view and I tried to imagine how the immigrants must have felt as they reached here, so close to the promised land but with no guarantee of entry. We disembarked with the rest of the passengers, but before joining any of the scheduled tours we took some time to wander around the building, looking at the vast halls where the ragged passengers would have waited to be processed, clutching their meagre possessions, hoping against hope that they would be given the opportunity to start a better life here. The cold I had felt on the trip over didn't leave me. I was chilled at the atmosphere of desperation and fear of being denied entry that still clung to the walls. I remembered the song Sean Keane had written after his visit to Ellis Island, "Isle of Hope, Isle of Tears". Its haunting melody played in my mind.

Later we went to the auditorium to watch a film on the history of the island. There were poignant scenes of the immigrants, who came mostly from Ireland, Italy, and Poland, undergoing medical checks. The sense of desperation felt by these people was palpable everywhere. They had fled extreme poverty and would have arrived here exhausted, sick, and malnourished. I felt immense respect for those who had made it by sheer will power and dogged determination.

'Let's go to the visitors' centre', Kathryn said. Here we would be able to research members of our family who had landed at Ellis Island. We paid for some time at one of the computer stations and trawled through some of the names of family from Ballinrobe. It was amazing to be able to see the original manifests on the screen, detailing the names and addresses of relatives, the date of their arrival, their contacts in America, and how much money they had with them. There was one John Feerick who had the princely sum of four shillings and tuppence on him.

After the Famine, the Irish continued to emigrate in search of a better life. My mother told of them leaving Ballinrobe:

One night I was at an American wake, that was so called in my young days because when the emigrant went to USA their parents would never see them again, so they always gave a big party the night before. It went on all night until it was time to wave them off to catch the boat at Cork.

We left the visitors' centre and walked towards the ferry. What we had experienced was also part of our heritage; it was humbling to learn more about this aspect of our culture and to realise how many of our forebears had undertaken the journey to Ellis Island in the hope of escaping adversity. *No wonder the Irish are such survivors,* I thought to myself. Kathryn and I spoke little on the way back. I gazed as Ellis Island disappeared from view, the mist enveloping it once more. We stood quietly on deck, holding the hand rail, alone with our thoughts.

That evening we went to a very fashionable Thai restaurant that had featured in the TV series *Sex and the City*. Mary's son David joined us. The food was delicious. We drank in the atmosphere, surrounded by glamorous New Yorkers. I was mesmerised at the outfits they wore: designer clothes in vibrant colours, full of bling, such a contrast to the drab rags of the immigrants whose photos we had viewed earlier that

Out on the town in New York

day. There was a frenzy of activity, with waiters shimmying between tables, holding large trays aloft, dodging their way through the crowds. I soaked in the atmosphere, feeling that I was well and truly in New York.

'How are book sales going?' Mary asked.

'Well', I replied.

'Any news from Liam about getting it into the Irish press?'

I explained the problems with distribution and that I was just not getting anywhere.

'But why don't you try Kenny's?' she asked.

'Who are they?'

'They are the biggest independent bookseller in Ireland. Until recently they had a large store in Galway, but they have closed it and are handling online ordering. Des Kenny also has a very popular book club; if you could just get in with that it would be useful. I'll try and get some contact details when I get home.'

'That would be such a help', I replied. 'It's been so frustrating; all I need is just one distributor.'

True to her word, Mary contacted me on her return to Ballinrobe with Des Kenny's details.

I sent him an email and received a prompt reply, asking for a copy of my book. Mary had some in Ballinrobe, so she sent one off. About ten days later I received a response. Des had enjoyed the book, but wasn't too sure how well it would sell, as the Irish content was limited. Still, I could send him ten copies on a sale-or-return basis and he would list it on his website.

I shot off emails to Mary and Kathryn to tell them the good news. I had distribution in Ireland! It would be enough to start working on some publicity with Liam. We chatted shortly afterwards.

'Hi Liam, I've managed to get my book listed with Kenny's. It will appear on their website in a couple of days and then I'll load the link on my own website, so we'll be up and running!'

'I'll start on a press release and as soon as it's done I'll be in touch. You can have a look at it and then we can discuss any changes.'

'I'm so pleased I've finally cracked it; I'll wait to hear from you.'

Finally some action. I knew there would be some interest in my story in the west of Ireland—it would probably be picked up by the *Mayo News*—but other than that, who knows? It was worth a try, anyway.

I arranged to send some books over to be kept in stock at Annie's house just in case there was a demand. Two days later I got a copy of Liam's press release. He had angled it more as a human-interest story than a book review. We adjusted a few minor details and it was ready to go.

'I'll let you know when I send it out', Liam said. 'You may receive calls from some journalists, so keep your phone on.'

A few days later I got an SMS from Kathryn: *Liam says keep your phone on—the release is out and there is already some interest.*

I kept my phone on but heard nothing. The next day I left my phone in the car while I went to the gym. When I returned to the car I saw that I had a text message from Kathryn. It read, *Mary says how many copies must she get?* I had no clue what she was talking about. I also had a voice-mail from a reporter from the *Mayo News*. I left a message. Then, as I was still in the gym car park, I logged on to my email, balancing my laptop on the passenger seat next to me with my wireless connection to see if there were any more messages. There was one from Kathryn explaining things. She said that there had been articles in several of the Irish daily tabloids: the *Sun, Mirror,* and *Mail.* She obviously wanted to know how many copies of each paper my cousin Mary needed to buy.

There was also an email from an RTE (the Irish national broadcaster) radio station in Dublin asking for an interview on *The Marian Finucane Show.* I phoned Liam quickly. 'Mary, some of the tabloids have run with your story. It's turning into something big, so please keep your phone on. I think there will be even more interest.'

I pulled out of the car park and headed for Grotto Bay on the N1 highway travelling north from Cape Town. My cell phone was on the passenger seat next to me, with the hands-free activated in case of any calls. It was mid-afternoon so there was not too much traffic, and I was able to focus on what was happening.

The phone rang. I glanced at the number, and noticed an Irish code. 'Hello, this is Rebekah Smith; I'm calling from *AM Live*. We'd like to know if you are planning a trip to Ireland to promote your book, as we'd like to invite you to appear on our breakfast TV show. You have such an incredible story.'

I was almost lost for words; it was so sudden. 'I haven't confirmed my dates yet', I replied, not wanting to discount the fact that this might well warrant a trip. I had no idea what this show was, nor if it was national or local. I asked her to send me an email as it was difficult to take down details while I was driving.

How about that for my first call? I thought to myself as I ended the call. A few minutes later, my phone rang again. This time it was the *Mayo News* requesting an interview. We arranged for them to phone me later that evening on my landline.

I continued on my way, approaching Century City shopping centre, a massive development on the side of the highway marked by pink and terracotta turrets. Yet another phone call: 'Hello, this is Fiona from *The Gerry Ryan Show*, RTE2. We'd like to know if you'd be interested in appearing on Gerry's show? Are you planning to come over here or could we interview you telephonically? Do you have an email address? I can hear you're driving, so I'll pop an email to you. Could you come back to me as soon as possible, please.'

Things were happening so quickly I decided to make a detour to Century City, where I could take a few minutes to check my email before continuing to Grotto Bay. It was a massive shopping mall but about the only place I could pull off safely and park. As I pulled into the parking lot the phone rang again. 'Hello, this is the *Irish Sunday Mail*. We'd like to interview you for our Sunday edition. We find your story compelling.' I gave them my landline number and suggested a convenient time for the interview.

I logged into my email again, my laptop balanced on my knees. I could see the person who pulled into the parking bay next to me giving me funny looks. I didn't care—I was too impatient to wait the forty-five minutes it would take me to drive home. I checked the new messages. There was the mail for the breakfast TV show and also for the *Gerry Ryan* and *Marian Finucane* shows. I phoned Liam and told him all about the calls and emails and got the background on the different shows. He led me through the details. The TV show and coverage on both *Gerry Ryan* and *Marian Finucane* was great, as Liam said it would give me the best possible exposure. He was pleased that I had been asked for additional print interviews as well.

'This is taking off', he said. 'Let's hope you have enough books in stock.' I sat in the car park replying to the emails for the TV and radio shows, all the time receiving calls from Irish local radio shows too. Finally I had dealt with everything. I just had to pop into the centre to pay for my parking. I looked at the slip. To my amazement I had been sitting in my car for two hours, fielding all these calls and emails. In the space of a few hours, so much had happened.

I continued my drive home, enjoying the peace and trying to take in the frenzy of media interest in my story. It was so unexpected, but very exciting. Hopefully none of the other drivers in the traffic were paying too much attention to me. I couldn't stop smiling, talking to myself. I was trying to assimilate what was happening. A car hooted at me to pull over and let him pass. As I pondered what was happening my speed had slowed; I hadn't realised it, and was holding up the BMW driver behind me. He flashed his lights at me as he sped past. Just one more call from Kilkenny Carlow radio station and then I was at Grotto Bay.

I got out of the car, inhaled the salty air, gazed at the sea, and tried to calm myself. I needed time to take everything in, but there was no time— my first interview was in barely half an hour. I paced around the house, trying to relax and slow down. It was like being on a roller coaster. I was wondering what questions I would be asked. I had had several months to relax since the interviews I had done for the South African media, and now it was starting again. Interviews were in some ways for me like having a session with a psychologist: all those probing questions, forcing me to confront and deal with all the issues from my past. It was good, therapeutic; it had helped me put many issues to rest.

I unpacked my laptop and set it up once again at the kitchen counter facing the sea. Just a couple more emails and there was Kathryn on the phone. She had read the mails I had forwarded her regarding the TV and radio shows and was very excited. I brought her up to speed about the other interviews and she told me about the articles in the Irish press, some of which she had managed to pick up in London from Eddie's newsagent in Cricklewood, where many Irish newspapers could be found. She planned to scan in the articles for me. I put the phone down with ten minutes to spare before the first interview of the evening, taking time to gather my thoughts and prepare myself for some of the questions they might ask.

By ten o'clock all the interviews were over. I phoned Kathryn to give her a rundown of how they'd gone before phoning Liam again. The interviewers had asked similar questions, all being shocked that John had just vanished, leaving me to work my way through the mess he had left. They were supportive and interested to know if I had managed to find him and how life was treating me now.

'I'm thinking it may be worth doing a trip over for the TV and radio shows', I told Liam. 'What do you think? Maybe I could fit in a book signing in Ballinrobe too.'

'That would be excellent, Mary. I could arrange some more interviews too, but just make sure it would translate into enough sales.'

'I know, that's the thing. I'll take a few days to see how things go. It has been quite a day. Thanks so much, Liam. Who could have imagined this would happen?'

'You have a great story, Mary, don't forget that. I'll probably chat to you tomorrow.'

I put the phone down and went out into the garden. I needed to walk to calm myself. I was too hyped up to sleep. Looking up at the stars in the crisp winter night and listening to the waves breaking on the rocks, I realised that Diane was right. My life was indeed changing as a result of the book. A chance to be interviewed on Irish TV and radio—what a proud moment! How I wished my parents were around to be part of this.

Chapter 10
A Great Irish Welcome

I had a marvellous time there.

The next day I went into my office, took the laptop out of my briefcase and logged on. I scanned the new emails quickly. I had been receiving several daily from people who had picked up on my story from the newspaper coverage and radio interviews. I was still getting used to the idea of complete strangers knowing the intimate details of my life and wishing to make personal contact. My story seemed to have taken on a life of its own. Yes, there were a couple more from unknown names, nothing too significant. I clicked on the last one. It was from someone called Tamsyn.

'Oh my God', I shrieked, 'I don't believe it!'

Who would have believed that after all these years Tamsyn would not only contact me, but offer to answer any questions I might have? She had left South Africa with John as they headed for Australia; the third woman in the equation, unbeknownst to both myself and Tracey, John's girlfriend in Richards Bay. Tamsyn had lived with him in Australia for all those years although they had now separated. I had wondered for so long about her: who was she, what was she like? What had John told her about me? Now she had approached me and was offering to answer the questions that had bugged me for so long.

I read and re-read the email. The writing of my book had set in motion so many unexpected events, and Tamsyn's message had unsettled me.

What could I say to her? How weird was it that we may now be in contact after all these years? I realised I needed time to get my head around this; I had to be careful how I worded my reply. Apparently the recent breakup between Tamsyn and John was not too amicable. I was suddenly having to confront things that had been far from my thoughts. I had of course known that Tamsyn existed, but I had chosen to ignore the fact, and bury it deep in the back of my mind. There was no reason for me to torment myself with thoughts of her relationship with John and of their life together in Australia. But now it obviously wasn't as simple as that. She had found me, she had now come into my life and was offering to answer my questions, but which questions should I ask?

I went outside into the office garden, where I walked around, talking to myself. It was a small space, but no matter—I needed to breathe the air, to still myself. Slowly the rhythm of my steps started to calm me. I looked up at the blue winter sky and saw a plane pass overhead. Watching distractedly as it faded into the distance, I continued to walk, occasionally picking up leaves from the wet grass and muttering to myself: *Why now? What should I ask? What is this all about?* Gradually I worked out what I was going to ask. In some ways I didn't want to know any more than I knew already. There was some merit in letting sleeping dogs lie, but fate had decided otherwise. For so many years my questions had been unanswered; I couldn't let this opportunity slip though my fingers.

I decided to limit myself to three or four questions. I didn't want to learn the details of Tamsyn's life with John; I simply wanted to know a few basic things. I respected Tamsyn for having the courage to contact me. She didn't have to do it and she had no idea what my reaction to her might be.

I crossed my fingers as I sent the email and then waited impatiently for her response. There wasn't much I wanted to know, just basic things like did she know about me? Her response came the next day. It was not as if we were cool with each other but there was a definite distance, which was understandable. She had answered my questions honestly and succinctly, there was no small talk or niceties, why would there be? I was glad that Tamsyn had contacted me but I knew that we would probably not contact each other again.

It felt strange and somewhat disconcerting to be in touch with someone who had been the cause of such heartache for me, albeit unwittingly. I knew it was John who had caused the pain, but Tamsyn was a part of it and her contact now served to raise my levels of unease dramatically. I had written my story from a position of strength, but now I was being reminded of my vulnerability. The publication of my book was to mark the beginning of a new stage in my life, but instead of putting those dreadful times to rest it was bringing them to the surface again. The most difficult chapter of my life was refusing to close.

I decided to go ahead with my plan to visit Ireland. I wanted to share my story not only as a way of healing myself, but as a way of encouraging others to move on with their lives. I contacted Liam to tell him of my plans and he asked for my itinerary. As soon as he had my dates he arranged to set up further interviews for me, beginning with Midwest Radio in Ballyhaunis. It was so appropriate to start everything off in the west of Ireland, close to Ballinrobe.

'The book signing is arranged for Martin Murphy's', my cousin Mary told me.

Doing a book signing in my cousin's shop felt just right. It had been part of our family history. I thought of the stories my mother had told me of her visits there to her cousin Jackie Murphy and how she would borrow newspapers, read them, iron them, and return them for resale as she could not afford to buy them. Now I was going to be signing my books in the very same shop. It brought a lump to my throat. It was all set up for the Friday after I arrived. Liam would send out a press release on the book signing to the local papers and I would also mention it on the radio.

All that remained was to arrange shipment of some books in time for the signing and to start planning my wardrobe. I wanted to look my best; this was such a significant trip for me.

'Why don't you rather print some books over there?' Diane asked.

'I haven't had a response from the printers or the distributors yet', I replied. 'When I wrote to them explaining that I had several interviews lined up and that there may be a market for my book in Ireland as a result, I was greeted by stony silence. I'll just have to resign myself to the fact that my book sales are going to be limited. It's so very frustrating', I told Diane.

'Watch', she said, 'just watch. You'll be such a hit; they'll be desperate to stock your book.'

'Let's hope so', I replied.

I wanted so much to reach the Irish market, but it seemed it wasn't going to be that easy. I decided to have a digital copy of the book with me on the trip. That way I'd be prepared. There just had to be a demand for my book. I knew it in my heart. All that remained was to convince the faceless distributors.

I started checking flights on the Internet. It was early summer in Europe, the high season, so prices were exorbitant. Still, I had made up my mind—this was something I had to do. It had been just a week since my story had hit the Irish press, and quite a week for me. I had done countless interviews and received emails from all over Ireland, with people expressing sorrow at my story and wishing me well. It was overwhelming to realise how deeply my personal account had touched people's hearts.

I landed at Shannon and drove to Ballinrobe through torrential rain, arriving there in the late afternoon. For most of the next day I was on the phone, chasing up the late arrival of my books, which should have been delivered to Annie well in advance of the book signing. It was Wednesday, the book signing was at Murphy's on Friday morning, and there was still no sign of them.

'Come and sit down', Annie said to me. 'I've made you some coffee, just relax. It will all get sorted out.' I sat in her front room, sipping my coffee and nibbling on a chocolate bar, feeling like a child again as I gazed at the familiar surroundings: the range, the picture of the Sacred Heart with the light in front of it, the clock in the corner with its weights hanging down. I was transported back to my teenage years when Kathryn, Mary, and I would come into this very front room after dances at the Ballinrobe Town Hall, to be summonsed into my aunt Annie and her husband Gerry's bedroom to report back. Who had we danced with? Had anyone walked us home? Those were happy, carefree days, and now here I was again, many years on, still being cared for, feeling the same love now. I felt calm again. Everything would work out the way it should.

'I need to phone Des Kenny too', I told Annie. 'Maybe I can go over to see him on Thursday afternoon. I know he needs books and I'd like to meet him. He has been so helpful and all this has happened because he decided to stock my book.' That was all Liam had needed to set the publicity in motion.

I finished my coffee and flopped back into the chair. It was going to be a whirlwind trip. I had only planned a few days in Ireland and it was looking like they would be filled to the brim.

I arranged to meet Des Kenny the following afternoon, as the books were due to arrive that morning. Then I left a message for Liam. He phoned back in the early evening and invited me for dinner at the local Chinese to go over things.

I walked down to the Chinese. It was lovely to be in Ireland in early summer; the evenings were already long and it was clear and mild. I was on familiar ground, walking the same road that I had been walking all my life, the houses unchanged, painted in a variety of colours, yellow, green. The lingering smell of turf fires clung to the air.

I got there before Liam and took a table in the corner. It was calm in the restaurant as it was still early. He arrived just a few minutes after me—a big, stocky man with a warm, friendly face. I had last seen him was when he was hosting a tour group in Cape Town and I had gone out with him for a meal in Camps Bay.

We chatted easily. He took me through the interviews he had set up and also the plan for the book signing. Liam had some more news for me, too: he had managed to arrange an exclusive interview with the English *Sunday Express*. The journalist would contact me to finalise a time and they would try and arrange a photo shoot for my day in London en route to South Africa. There was so much happening, it was hard to take it all in.

The next morning, just I was about to set out for Midwest Radio in Ballyhaunis and my interview on *The Tommy Marren Show*, the weather took a turn for the worse. Fortunately I had planned for rain when I packed and I grabbed my umbrella and coat.

'I think I'd better go now', I said to Mary. 'I have to pick up your mum in time to get to the radio station.'

'No problem. See you later.'

As I drove to Annie's house in Glebe Street I listened to the radio. Pulling up outside her gate I heard them say, 'Coming up in *The Tommy Marren Show*, an interview with Mary Monaghan, author of *Remember Me?*' I smiled to myself. Here I was in Ballinrobe, setting off for an interview on Irish radio with Annie in tow; it was going to be such fun.

Annie rushed to the car, clutching two umbrellas in case I had forgotten mine. We chatted happily as I drove the back roads to Ballyhaunis. *The west of Ireland is so beautiful*, I thought as we passed the gently rolling green hills, stone walls, and fuchsia hedges in full bloom. Annie gave me all the background on Midwest Radio and the presenters. She was excited to be joining me on this expedition and I was happy to have her with me. It was very comforting being with family, something I missed in South Africa.

We waited for Tommy to collect us from reception. In a few minutes we heard him chatting in the passageway to one of his assistants and then he came out to meet us: a tall, sandy-haired man with an easy manner and an engaging smile. 'I couldn't resist introducing the interview with "Save Your Kisses for Me" by Brotherhood of Man', he laughed. 'I thought it was very appropriate.'

'You're so right', I replied.

'Let's go in. I'm sure you're used to doing interviews so we'll just chat along, if that's OK?'

'Is it possible for my aunt to sit in?'

'Of course—we'll have a chair for her in the corner.'

We settled into the interview. Tommy was obviously interested in my links to Ballinrobe, so many of the questions revolved around my Irish roots. But he also had insightful questions about my story. Towards the end of the interview he asked me a question that had often been on my mind.

'What would you do if you saw John again? Would you like to meet up with him again?'

I had no pat answer for him.

'Part of me would like to see him again and part of me wouldn't at all. In some ways it would be good to have some form of closure, but I know that if I saw him again it would bring back all the hurt and pain and I'm not sure I want to relive that.'

'Yes, I imagine there must always be a level of hurt deep down.'

'Yes, there most certainly is.'

We chatted further and Tommy gave details of the book signing before closing off. It was a lovely interview. I felt very at ease. I had so wanted it to go well. I was glad that Annie had been part of it, sitting in the corner taking everything in, smiling at my responses. It was wonderful to have her there with me. Although I could only see her out of the corner of my eye, I could feel her support. This was the first time anyone had been with me when I was interviewed; usually I was on my own.

Tommy arranged for us to get a CD of the interview an hour later, so we went to the local coffee shop for a hearty Irish breakfast before going back to Ballinrobe. As we sat at the table my cell phone kept buzzing with messages from Kathryn and my cousins, who had listened in via audio-streaming in London. I was ravenous and tucked in to the feast of eggs, bacon, sausage, and black pudding.

As soon as we finished breakfast I got on the phone again to the courier company. The books had still not been delivered. They promised to phone me back within the hour. The situation was becoming desperate. What was the purpose of a book signing if there were no books to sign? An hour later I did indeed receive a call: the books would be in Galway that afternoon and then they would deliver to me early the next morning. I was furious: that just wasn't good enough. I couldn't leave it until the last minute. I was due to visit Kenny's that afternoon in Galway, so I told the couriers I would pick the books up there.

Des Kenny greeted me warmly, wanting to know about my plans for the trip and wishing me well with my interviews and book signing. I signed some copies for him and he explained that he had already sent some copies to members of his book club in the United States.

The courier van was due to arrive in the late afternoon, in the middle of the rush hour. The man from the courier company suggested we meet on the outskirts of town. He would give me directions. I left my meeting at four o'clock and negotiated the one-way system around Galway, battling through the traffic and torrential rain. This was not what I had planned, I thought to myself. I had allowed plenty of time, but this was becoming a nightmare.

Several wrong turns later, I reached the parking lot we had agreed on for our rendezvous. Thank goodness, there was a white van there. As I pulled in the driver flashed his lights at me. Despite all the stress of the situation, I giggled; it felt like something out of a film: an illicit meeting in a parking lot to transfer goods, it looked so suspicious. I jumped out of the car, oblivious to the rain and mud. I was on a mission, I just wanted my books. Nothing else mattered. There they were, parcelled up in the back of the van. I signed the documents, loaded the books in the boot and sat for a few minutes in the car trying to dry off, remove the mud spatters from my skirt, and recover my composure. What a close call! But I had my books, and that was all that mattered.

The next day I was due to do the book signing at Murphy's on Main Street.

'What time does it start?' Mary asked.

'It starts at 11 AM but I plan to get there at about 10:15 to set things up and make sure everything is ready.'

'I'm glad you managed to get the books eventually.'

'So am I. What a relief! But I can't believe I had to drive all the way to Galway in the pouring rain to get them in time for the signing.'

'Better late than never. You look great!'

'Thanks, I wanted to wear something comfortable but a little bit different. I need to look good for the photos!'

'Talking of which, here's my camera; there's loads of memory available, so don't hold back.'

I packed some extra books into the boot of the car and set off for town. It was difficult to gauge how many I would need, and I had already dropped some copies off with my cousin Martin Murphy. I parked close to the shop, so that if I needed extra books they would be close at hand. We had done as much publicity as we could, but I couldn't anticipate what the response would be.

I walked into Murphy's, noticing big posters advertising my book in the window. The shop had a bit of everything: newspapers, books, CDs, jewellery. The book display was already set up in a corner near the jewellery so as not to clutter the main part of the shop. In front of it was a table for the signing. Solange, the young Brazilian shop assistant, had a designated till set up for book sales. Everything was very organised.

Half an hour before the official start time I had my first sale, to the lady from the local library. Just as she arrived so did Annie, who sat down next to me. We had planned that she would introduce me to people; there were so many familiar faces, but sometimes I battled with names. From eleven o'clock people just kept coming. There was a constant buzz around the table, with old friends chatting together while they waited in line. It was good to see them all there, and many put in a kind word, recounting their memories of me as a little girl or talking about my parents.

I needn't have worried about the signing being a flop; people were queuing for me to sign. I met a priest from Australia who was buying a copy for his mother. Like several other people there, he had heard me on the radio. Some had even read my book already and had brought in their used copy. It gave me particular satisfaction to sign a dog-eared copy.

As the morning went on I realised that I needed to replenish the stock of books, so Martin ran out to the car to get some more. At that moment I saw Liam in the doorway; he couldn't make it through the crowds of people so he just gave me the thumbs up and went on his way. It had turned out better than any of us could have imagined.

We were well over time and gradually things were slowing down. Martin asked me if I would be passing Charlestown on my way to Dublin on Saturday. I explained that I would be going that way, but not until Sunday as I had planned to go to Donegal on Saturday.

'That's a shame', Martin said. 'I've had a call from someone from Mayo/Roscommon Hospice looking for a copy of your book for the raffle, but she needs it by Saturday. Here's her number anyway. Maybe you can phone her.'

We started to pack up the last of the books. The occasion had been such fun, and a resounding success. All the time I was there I felt my parents' presence with me, as the signing took place in their home town surrounded by so many of their family and friends. I still missed them so much but had felt them with me all the time, guiding and watching over me. It gave me endless satisfaction to be there. I had come home in a way, and my journey had brought me full circle and back to my roots. The sadness at what had led me to write my book was far outweighed by the satisfaction of putting it to good use and sharing my experience with others. I felt that both my parents would have been happy that

Book signing in Ballinrobe

I had brought my book home.

My cousin Mary arrived and helped me pack the car. I explained that I had called the lady from the Mayo/Roscommon Hospice, Ann Meehan, and had decided to take a drive out that way.

'It's a fair distance', Mary said.

'I know, but I feel like taking a drive. There's been so much going on. I need some time just to gather my thoughts, especially as I'll be rushing around tomorrow, dropping off books in Donegal, Sligo, and Ballyshannon. I know it will be stressful visiting John's home town. I've never been there before and somehow it seems to be bringing everything too close for comfort.'

'Yes, I imagine it will be. Will you be seeing his aunt Elizabeth this time?'

'Yes, I've arranged to meet her for lunch. She was such a good and loyal friend to me through those years, and after all, it was through her that I finally managed to find John. But I still find it upsetting and un-settling to be with her.'

'Take time for yourself', Mary advised. 'There won't be much of that for the next few days.'

She was right. Just as I got into the car I received a call from Rebekah Smith, wanting to go through some of the questions they planned to ask me on the breakfast TV show on Monday. There was nothing too unusual: *Why did you wait so long for him to come back? Have you had any further contact with him since your last phone call?* It was all very standard. I confirmed that since I had tracked John down six years after he left for Australia, there had been no further contact. It had been fourteen years since I had last seen him leave our house in South Africa to go backpack-ing in Australia, so there was slim chance of my ever seeing him again and that was just fine.

On the way back from Charlestown I stopped at Knock to visit Our Lady's shrine. There was an RTE TV broadcast van there filming a vigil for Madeline McCann, the young girl who had gone missing in Portugal. I could empathise with the pain of her parents, anxious to find out what had happened to her, desperately searching for answers. I went to a side chapel to avoid the crowds. There I lit a candle and sat quietly, trying to allow the stillness to calm and slow me down. So much had happened already, so many interviews, raising old hurts. I just knew going to John's home town would be stressful. My trip was raising memories I had thought were long erased. I felt close to John here in Ireland, it was part of who he was and what had shaped him. Meeting his aunt Elizabeth was always a reminder of the dark days when I was searching for him. I sat for about twenty minutes, slowing my breathing, feeling the silence, until I felt calmer and more settled. I knew all would be well.

Chapter 11

Full Circle

Little did she know what shock was in store for her.

The next morning I pulled out of Mary's driveway, closing the gate behind me. I glanced at the back seat to check that I had enough books for my deliveries in Donegal and Sligo. *Thank goodness the weather is holding up,* I thought to myself. It wasn't all that warm, but it looked as though it was going to be dry at least. I had planned these trips well, going on the Internet and making sure that I had printed out the routes for my journey. Normally when I went to Ireland, Kathryn did the driving, so I didn't pay too much attention to where I was going. This time it was different; I had hired a car and was enjoying my independence.

As I left Ballinrobe early that June morning I turned on the radio and tried to prepare myself for the day ahead. Midwest Radio was playing familiar songs—songs I used to hear at the Galtymore Irish club in Cricklewood when I was still single. It brought back memories of those days in London, my early days with John. It had been fourteen years since I had seen him. For six of those years I hadn't known if he was alive or dead, where he was, or if he intended coming back. A deep sense of sadness enveloped me: so many wasted years. How could someone I had loved so much hurt me so badly?

I checked the address for the book store in Sligo and finally found the shop after several detours. As I moved out of the parking lot I found myself driving the wrong way up a one-way street and was promptly pulled over by a Garda on duty to manage the traffic flow. I explained that I lived in South Africa, apologising profusely, and he let me off with a warning.

Now it was off to Donegal. Ballyshannon, John's home town, was on the way. I would have lunch there with Elizabeth on my way back to Ballinrobe. It had been some time since I had seen her; we had talked over the phone after I had published my book, but it would be good to spend some time with her now face to face. So much had happened since we had last met.

I found the book shop in Donegal very easily. What I couldn't find was parking, and to make matters worse, it had started raining. In my rush to leave the house that morning I hadn't thought to grab an umbrella. I decided to leave the Donegal delivery. The traffic was just too bad and parking was a nightmare. I had forgotten to factor in the Saturday morning rush in my time estimates. I muttered impatiently as another driver pulled out in front of me. *Calm down,* I said to myself. *Relax, don't get stressed about meeting Elizabeth, take it easy.*

"I'll Take You Home Again Kathleen" played on the radio. My eyes filled with tears—it was the song my father always sang to my mother. I found a place to stop the car, closed my eyes, and lay back in the seat, letting the song weave its way into my thoughts. I started to feel calmer; it was as if my parents were there with me, watching over me. I had had a strange feeling all day; it must be the thought of being in John's home town. I was nervous, my stomach was in knots. I was more emotional than I had been for years. I probably should have stayed away from Ballyshannon. Why put myself through this? I felt vulnerable. I had never been here before, never visited John's home. Why come to his home town now? My trip to Ireland was surfacing so many emotions.

Just as I was pulling out of the parking area, Elizabeth phoned. 'Are you on your way yet?'

'Yes, I'm just leaving. I'll be there in twenty minutes. I'll drop off the books and then we can catch up over lunch.' I felt more than able to meet her now; I was over my brief panic attack and felt strong again.

'Where shall I meet you?'

'How about outside the book shop, after you've done your business there?'

I had seen the shop, A Novel Idea, earlier on my way through Ballyshannon; all I had to do was find parking. As I approached the shop a space opened up just in front. *Thank goodness, that was easy,* I thought as I manoeuvred my way into the space. After adjusting my hair and freshening my lipstick, I got out of the car and opened the

A Novel Idea

boot to get the books. Then I walked into the shop, making my way through the post office at the front towards the stationery and book shop at the back. The shop was packed to the brim with things; there was very little space to move between the aisles. I had seen a handwritten notice in the front window advertising my books for sale and had brought some posters with me, which they could now use instead.

The owner of the shop came up to greet me. She was glad to receive more copies, as they had already run out. There had been a high demand for my books in the town. So many people knew John and his family, and were intrigued to read the story of what had happened.

'Enjoy your stay in Ireland; I'm looking forward to seeing you on TV on Monday', the shop owner said as I left after signing some copies for her.

I got back in the car. Just at that moment, I saw Elizabeth drive by, looking for parking. I waved at her to show her I was there. She indicated that she would circle again. I looked in the rear-view mirror a little later and saw Elizabeth pull into a parking bay about three cars behind me. I watched her get out of the car: a short blonde woman, dressed in jeans and a denim shirt. I grabbed my bag from the passenger seat, eased out of my own car, and began walking towards her. It was great to see Elizabeth; she was looking good even at a distance. She had hardly changed since I had first met her in London over twenty years before.

Suddenly John was there, right in front of her.

I stopped dead in my tracks, put my hands up to my face and stood stock still. John kept walking towards me. I turned my back to him and remained rooted to the spot. I didn't move, I didn't speak, I didn't know what to do. I was too stunned. He reached me as I stood there, my hands still covering my face in total shock. There he was, John, looking as he always did: older, of course, but still the very John with whom I had fallen in love all those years ago.

'Hello Mary', he said softly.

I couldn't speak—I, who am so rarely lost for words. My hands still covered my face, my lips couldn't move, my body felt like stone. There must have been a look of horror on my face.

Elizabeth eventually broke the ice.

'I think you should go over to Dorrian's Hotel and have a chat.'

I was still mute. John spoke again. 'You don't have to come if you don't want to', he said.

I looked at him and said, 'It's fine'.

'I'll be there in a little while; take as much time as you like', Elizabeth told us.

John led the way to the hotel; I followed him in silence, crossing the road blindly, unaware of any traffic that might be passing. My hands had dropped to my sides, but still I could not speak. I felt numb, dazed, as if I was sleepwalking. After all those years, how do you pick up a conversation? Where do you start? All my planned scenarios had involved me surprising John, not the other way around. He had caught me on the back foot. We went into the bar.

'Will you have a drink?' he asked.

'A dry white wine, please', I answered. I knew it was only half past eleven but after the shock I needed fortification.

I glanced around the pub. No one in sight; it was too early for customers. I sat down in a secluded area, trying to ignore the smell of stale wine and beer. It was difficult to think of having a conversation with John after all these years, and in such a public place. I knew I had to keep myself together but realised that it was going to be easier said than done.

I adjusted myself in the chair; I

Dorrian's Hotel

couldn't seem to get comfortable. I crossed and uncrossed my legs, waiting for John to come back and join me. I was glad I'd decided to wear something casual: jeans and a top. I felt good in them and they were easy to wear. Right now nothing else felt right; the situation was so awkward.

John seemed to take an age at the bar. I took the opportunity to size him up from a distance. He hadn't changed that much at all. His hair was pretty much the same, not too grey yet; it had receded, though. He was wearing jeans and a white shirt, hanging loosely over his jeans. Still the same John.

He carried two small bottles of wine and glasses back to the table.

'I'm afraid the choice of wine here isn't that good', he said. 'Not like the South African and Australian wines we're used to.'

'That's for sure', I replied.

John looked up at me with his blue eyes, registering all the emotion in my face. I still couldn't find it in me to speak. After all this time, I just didn't know what to say. He looked at me again; his face was pale and strained. He spoke so softly it was hard to hear what he was saying. I felt myself move closer to hear him better.

'I walked right into this', John said, still looking at me. 'I had no idea.'

'I didn't know you were here', I replied, waiting patiently for him to start the real conversation.

'I came for a week to see my parents and now I'm seeing my face in all the newspapers. Every time I go into the pub in Cashelard people come up and say "Remember me?" I feel like I'm on trial.'

'I had no idea there'd be this level of interest in my book. Have you read it?'

'No I haven't, but my mother has.'

'I would have sent you a copy but I didn't know where you were. I heard that you'd moved and no one had a new address for you.'

'I didn't move.'

'That's strange; I wonder what gave them the idea?'

'Tamsyn and I broke up; maybe that's why.'

'Did you ever think I would write a book?'

'I always knew you would. Your mother always said she would write a book and you're so like your mother.'

How strange that he would remember that, I thought. John and my mother had been very close: they had got on well when she came to visit us in Johannesburg in 1988. She was busy writing her journal, *Green Are the Hills Far Away*, at the time. She died just a few months later.

Still we skirted the real issue, making small talk. John had decided to surprise me on my visit to Ballyshannon, when he had heard through the local grapevine that I was going to be at the book shop. It was up to him now to say what he had come to say. I waited for him to start speaking. I wasn't going to make it easier for him, he owed me an explanation. Here was his opportunity to do the right thing and he was going to have to do it with no help from me. I clenched a tissue tightly in my hand. While John was at the bar I had made sure I had tissues easily to hand. My eyes filled with tears periodically. I wiped them away each time and composed myself until the next wave of emotions. John looked at me as I dabbed at my eyes.

'I thought you had got over me', he said. 'You've moved on.'

'I have', I replied. 'But seeing you again brings back all the hurt.'

'I never meant to hurt you; it was just so difficult. You have no idea how bad things were for me. I wanted to contact you but I couldn't. I picked up the phone so many times.'

'So why didn't you?'

'It was like a breakdown—I went into a black hole.'

'And you couldn't write to me, just one line to say you weren't coming back?'

'It wasn't that simple; I didn't know what to say.'

'Did you realise what this did to me?'

'Of course, I always have. There's not a day goes by that I don't think of you.'

'But you didn't contact me.'

'I know, I should have.'

'Why did you decide to come and see me today?'

'I had to; it was the right thing to do. My mother encouraged me. You've been hard on my mother. She did what she thought was the best thing to do.'

'So it was right to know where you were and, despite her promise to me, to keep the information from me for over a year?'

'She understands now that it was wrong. She read your book and said

I should see you.'

'I have a copy in the car. Will you read it?

'I don't know. I saw a psychologist in Australia after the breakup with Tamsyn and she suggested that I write a book about what happened between us.'

'Well I've done it for you. It's not vindictive; in fact many people have said I've been too nice. It'll give you an idea of how things were for me.'

'You might not have written it vindictively, but I know I've become a hate figure for many women.'

'Maybe you have, but that was never my intention.'

'Men seem to have a different take on things. Some have come up to me in the pub and shaken my hand, saying, "Thank goodness there are still some real men left!"' He grinned at me.

I looked at him, this stranger sitting in front of me, this man I thought I loved, and realised what kind of a man he was. It seemed he didn't feel that bad about what he had done, that it had been in some way excusable. In some perverse way he felt it had affirmed his masculinity.

This was the man who had caused me such heartache, whom I had loved so much. I was sitting across the table from him and I didn't even want to reach for his hand. I felt no desire to touch him. How could it be that a man for whom I had felt so much passion could leave me so cold? We were so close and yet so very far apart.

Elizabeth appeared at the door of the lounge bar and waved. 'My friend is asking if she can have a photo taken with you', she called.

'I'll be there right now', I said, getting up from the chair, welcoming the breather from my conversation with John.

I posed for a couple of photos and chatted with Elizabeth's friend. Elizabeth took my hand, checking that I was coping. I assured her I was fine and that I wouldn't be much longer, and then headed back to John.

'You're quite the celebrity, aren't you?' he said.

I listened as he told me of his new business venture in Uruguay. John was still very much the businessman; it was all about doing deals, and far less about people. *Hindsight is such a thing*, I thought. These indications of the man John was should have served as a warning bell all those years previously.

I began to feel more composed. I was getting through this. I hated the fact that I had cried earlier, not from weakness, but just from the years of emotion that seeing him had brought to the surface.

'I have a television interview booked for Monday. They're bound to ask me if I've seen you', I said.

'Just tell them whatever you want to tell them. I'm a businessman, you're a businesswoman, you're here to promote your book.'

'It's not about promoting my book; it's about being honest. I can't lie to them.'

'Do what you have to. I suppose you'll write another book after this.'

'Maybe I will, but for the moment I am turning the book into a screenplay. Everyone says it will make a good film.'

'So who would play me?'

'Goodness knows.'

'I think it should be Brad Pitt.'

I could see John was serious; he wasn't fazed at the thought of a film being made of our story.

I noticed Elizabeth waiting patiently in the lobby of the hotel. Looking at my watch, I realised that I had kept her waiting far too long. John and I had nothing more to say to each other.

'I'll have to join Elizabeth', I said. 'It's not fair to keep her waiting like this, as she is the reason I came here.'

'I'll be in touch, Mary', he said.

'Where have I heard that before?' I retorted. I just couldn't help myself.

'I will be. I did contact you again after your phone call. I sent you a letter.'

'I never got it. When did you send it?'

'About a year or so after we spoke.'

'A year or so? Even if I had got it don't you think that was a little too long?'

'I know, I just couldn't seem to find the words.'

'So why should I believe this time will be different?'

'It will be', John replied.

'OK, here are my contact details. I'll wait to hear from you. Please give me yours too.'

He handed me a card.

'You'll hear from me soon', he said.

'How soon?'

'Within a month', he replied.

'OK, let's shake on that.'

I looked at him. Did I believe him? No, I didn't, but I would give him the benefit of the doubt.

John stood up to leave. I watched him go with mixed emotions: sadness, anger, and the satisfaction of realising that I was in control of my life. By contrast, John seemed to be all over the place. As he spoke about his plans he didn't seem confident; he jumped from one thing to another, never fully explaining what he was busy with. Throughout our conversation he had found it hard to look me in the eye. He seemed strained, ill at ease—hardly surprising, I suppose, given the circumstances.

Elizabeth joined me in the bar.

'Are you OK?' she asked.

'Yes, I'm fine—emotional, but I'll be all right.'

'Let's go and have some lunch.'

We left the bar and went over the road to the coffee shop. We chatted over a light lunch, but I was distracted. It was good to see Elizabeth again, but all I wanted to do was get into my car and gather my thoughts. Before heading back to Ballinrobe we passed by her pretty little cottage and she showed me around. It was lovely, but I was absent-minded in my praise for it. My head was spinning with all that had happened. I felt distant, preoccupied. I kept seeing John's face and hearing his voice.

I eventually said my goodbyes and took the road out of town. I felt bad that I had short-changed Elizabeth, hardly spending time with her, but I desperately needed time to myself to reflect on what had happened and my reactions to it.

I had a splitting headache. All the tension of the last few hours was clearly evident. I talked to myself as I drove, trying to make sense of it all. I had almost felt sorry for John. He was not in good shape emotionally. I felt so much more under control: a book under my belt, media interviews scheduled, and compassion from others for my story. I pulled off the road once I felt calm and phoned Kathryn. I spoke to her briefly, telling her what had just happened, putting her worries to rest, reassuring her that I was fine and just needed some time. She was concerned that John would get the better of me, wheedle his way back into my affections, wear me down, but I assured her there was definitely no chance of that.

I had already arranged an evening out with Mary and Annie before I left for Dublin the next day. As I approached Ballinrobe I decided to detour towards the lake and Cahir Pier, a place I had often visited with my parents. I wanted to experience some stillness before sharing the news with everyone; some privacy before too many people got to know what had happened. This was a very personal thing and I needed time to gather my thoughts.

I drove down the windy lane to the lake, parking to the side before getting out of the car. As my legs touched the ground they buckled and I had to hold on to the door for support. My legs were shaking so badly I could hardly walk. I hadn't realised how stressed I was until then. I walked up and down, trying to calm myself. Eventually I sat down at the lake, gazing at the sun on the water, thinking of my parents.

Slowly, calm was restored to me. I took out my phone and tapped out a very short message to my friends. *Just bumped into John in Ballyshannon. We had a talk, all's well. Chat soon.* I needed them to know, they deserved that, but I just didn't feel like going into more detail just yet. They would understand that I would tell them more when I got back.

I sat deep in thought for another few minutes. I knew it would be a rush to get ready for dinner, but I needed the stillness to envelop me. I threw a few stones in the water, watching the ripples on the surface of the lake as I said a short prayer of thanks for what had just been. My book had led me back to John; indeed, it had changed my life. I looked up at the sky and smiled. *It's done. I've seen John and I'm just fine.*

Cahir Pier, Lough Mask

Chapter 12

Our Story Continues ...

I felt at peace.

I arrived at Annie's a little while later, rushing in the door as I was now running late.

'There's something I need to tell you.'

'What's that?' Annie replied. 'How was your trip?'

'It was good, but you won't believe what happened. I ran into John.'

'You did? Oh my goodness—are you OK?'

'I'm fine, I am.'

'What happened? Tell me all about it. I'll put the kettle on and make you some coffee. You must eat something too—you must be shattered.' Annie busied herself in the kitchen, preparing coffee and biscuits before joining me in the front room.

I pulled my chair closer to the table, rested my head on my hands, and started to tell Annie all about my meeting with John; it was a story that would be told over and over in the next few days. I told it to Annie almost dispassionately. I felt very in control—or was I? I knew I had a busy few days ahead; I was leaving for Dublin the next day. I had a telephonic interview scheduled for a feature in the *Sunday Express,* then on Monday the breakfast TV show and *The Gerry Ryan Show* on Tuesday. There was no time to go to pieces. I needed to be on top of things in the next few days; then the tears could flow later. The last thing I needed now was to be a basket case for the interviews.

Besides, in a way, after the initial moments of disbelief, horror, and shock, meeting John had been an anticlimax. Despite all these emotions I had a strong sense of how stupid it had been to waste so many good years of my life over him. There was no doubt, though, how traumatic it had been: sitting across the table from the man who had caused me so much heartache and for whom, despite everything, I would always have a special place in my heart.

While John had sat in front of me, I had thought to myself, *What was the big deal after all?* The flaws I had seen in the years following his departure had become all too apparent now; I had wasted so much of my life on someone who hadn't deserved my love. Now it was about me, and I was going to show everyone that I was strong and a survivor. I was no longer a victim in all of this; I had already taken charge by writing my book, and was not going to relinquish that position. There was no way I was going to allow John to change that.

As I·was talking to Annie, an SMS came through on my mobile—it was Liam. I had told him the news and needed advice as to how to handle the TV interview on Monday and the radio interviews after that. Did I need to tell them what had happened, or should I reply only to a direct question? Liam arranged to come to Mary's house early the next morning to go through things and to prepare a press release for distribution once I had told my story on TV.

'You should tell the TV interviewers before you go on air', he advised. 'It's only fair.'

'OK', I replied. 'I just know it will cause a stir.'

'I know', Liam replied, 'but don't worry; I'll prepare something for the newspapers, that way it will take the heat off you. Just take me through what happened, then I'll put something together and email it to you. Will you have email access at the hotel?'

'Yes, apparently so.'

'Then that's fine; you'll have time to review it before Monday. Please also tell Ciara from the *Sunday Express* what happened. Her story is only due out a week later anyway.'

'OK, thanks for all your help; this has spiralled out of control. Who would have thought we would be having this conversation?'

'Indeed, it was obviously meant to be.'

I saw Liam to the door and then went up to my room to do the last of the packing. I wanted to get to Dublin in good time so that I would be well settled in the hotel before the journalist phoned. Then I'd have an hour or two to relax before Kathryn arrived from the airport. She was flying in from a music competition in Scotland and was due later that evening. She would be coming to the TV studio with me the next morning. I knew Kathryn would be anxious to see if I was all right after my meeting with John. I glanced at the room: clothes all over the place, on the floor, on the bed, hanging on the wardrobe door, reds mingling with browns. I needed to get some order into all of this. I had packed for every eventuality; now I had to somehow fit it all back into my case.

Before I left I sent a brief text message to John. I somehow needed to acknowledge his finally having the courage to contact me. His reply came back immediately.

Thanks—too little too late.

I smiled. He was exactly right; I couldn't have said it better myself.

I said goodbye to Mary and then drove into Ballinrobe to say goodbye to Annie. She gave me a big hug and wished me all the best for the interviews. I told her I would phone her as I went along to let her know how things were going. She waved me off as I set off down Glebe Street. I checked the mirror and watched her standing there waiting for me to disappear from view, her hand now dropping to her side as she went inside. I caught myself sighing, a small sigh, a mixture of contentment at the familiarity of things and an acknowledgment that I was now on my own once more.

I drove out of Ballinrobe, enjoying the tranquillity of the open road. I'd had little time to myself since meeting John, and I was looking forward to having some space to reflect on what had happened and to prepare for what lay ahead. How could I answer the inevitable questions about my meeting with John when I hadn't even processed them correctly in my own mind? It had all been so sudden, my head was still spinning. Where did I stand on all of this? I felt sadness, coldness, sorrow. Had I been too rough on him, had I taken my book too far? It was a whole different ball game now that I had met him face to face; the event had knocked me off balance.

I looked out at the grey sky. It may have been early summer, but the temperature was more like a Cape Town winter's day. I hoped the rain would hold off, at least. I glanced at the AA route instructions to Dublin Airport. It seemed simple enough and I was making good time. I passed a few tractors lumbering up the hills loaded with hay, and returned the waves of the farmers as they motioned me to pass. It then became slow going as I started to encounter sheep on the road. I slowed down almost to a standstill, edging slowly forward, smiling as their black faces almost challenged me to leave them alone; then slowly, slowly they parted, giving me enough space to get through, *baa*-ing at me, noting their displeasure that I had encroached on their space.

I was just a few miles from the airport when the traffic ground to a halt. We were at a standstill and remained like this for over thirty minutes. Then the traffic started to crawl along, obviously not fast enough for some travellers, who leapt out of their transport and made their way to the terminal building on foot. I looked at my watch. This was taking forever, and I would be at the hotel barely in time for my interview. So much for allowing calmness to descend. I was feeling more frantic than ever.

Just as I had the terminal buildings in my sights, my friend Liam O'Brien from Connecticut phoned to see how I was doing. We had become friends when I met him on one of his annual trips to Cape Town, where he and his students were filming a documentary. A professor at Quinnipiac University in Connecticut, Laim taught screenwriting. He had offered to guide me in the writing of the screenplay adaptation of my book.

Liam heard the edge of hysteria in my voice as the minutes ticked away and I was no nearer the airport. I had thought I was all right but my level of control was obviously very superficial—there was a vast degree of stress bubbling under the surface. For the first time since meeting John, I truly broke down. Liam didn't wait too long on the phone, just long enough to calm me down, wish me luck for the interviews, and tell me to take care of myself.

I finally pulled into the car rental parking lot, only to be confronted by a lengthy queue of stressed travellers who had all been held up in the traffic jam. My relaxing day had definitely gone for a ball of chalk. Eventually I dealt with all the paperwork and boarded the shuttle for the hotel. I should still be in time for the interview and have some relaxation time before Kathryn arrived, so all was well, or so it seemed.

The bus route took us past Croke Park just as a big football match was finishing, so once again I sat in a traffic jam. I started chatting to a young girl who was sitting next to me; she looked nervous and was reading and rereading a two-page document. She explained that it was information for a job interview the next day. I assured her it would be fine and exchanged details of what I was going to be up to the next day. We told each other we would be fabulous!

I kept looking at my watch; timing was very tight. Just at that moment my phone rang. It was Ciara, confirming the interview. I explained the traffic problems and we agreed to postpone it by an hour. That would give me just about enough time.

There's the hotel! I jumped off the bus and made my way to reception. Thankfully check-in was very efficient. I bought my Internet token and went back to the room. As city hotels go it wasn't too bad: twin beds, a reasonably sized bathroom, and plenty of wardrobe space. I hurriedly hung up my outfit for the TV interview the next day and got out all my accessories: jewellery, shoes, handbag. I wanted to be sure that all was taken care of. After arranging my toiletries in the bathroom, I kicked off my shoes, sat on the edge of the bed, and closed my eyes for just a brief moment before the phone rang. It was Ciara.

She confirmed that I was OK to talk and then interviewed me for almost one and a half hours. Where did I meet John? What had attracted me to him? And of course the inevitable questions once I had told her of my chance meeting with John: How did I feel? Was I still in love with him? In some ways it was good to be asked all these things. It forced me to confront issues that I would happily have left alone.

I put the phone down, leant back in the chair, and closed my eyes, feeling drained. I could hear the sound of the television in the next room. It sounded like an action film, lots of gunfire and shouting. I knew that writing my book would expose me and my story to so many people, but I hadn't anticipated the volume of interest or that I would be expected to share my current story. That had never been part of the plan. Now, of course, it had become inevitable.

I pulled myself up out of the chair and went to the bathroom to run myself a bath, my standard remedy for stress. I switched on the TV—a music show, the Princess Diana Memorial Concert. It was perfect, some music to listen to while I soaked away the rigours of the day. I lay in the bath for almost an hour, inhaling the smell of the camomile oil I had put in the water, topping up regularly with hot water, monitoring Kathryn's progress by the text messages she kept sending me. Kathryn too was stuck in traffic. I felt the tension slowly drift away from my body; my legs felt heavy, my head felt clear.

I got out of the bath feeling refreshed. I put on some comfortable clothes, and headed down to the restaurant. I wasn't sure what time it closed and wanted to make sure I could arrange food for Kathryn if need be. She was going to meet me there as soon as she got to the hotel. I sat in a cosy nook in the pub area and continued to watch the concert while I waited.

In between I did some people-watching. There were mostly tourists, rushing in with shopping bags, anxious to grab something to eat before the restaurant closed. I made out a mixture of languages: German, Spanish, Italian, and Dutch mixed in with some English and American accents. I watched a young family make its way to one of the alcoves. The mother hardly made it to the seat, collapsing with a heap of shopping bags around her. Her children started to run riot around the dining area until the father summoned up the energy to chase after them and settle them down with some stern words. The noise levels were high, between the substantial number of children, two televisions blaring out the concert, and people shouting to be heard. I made a determined effort to think calm thoughts.

Eventually Kathryn arrived, just in time to order a pub supper. We had so much to talk about. It was going to be lovely to have her with me when I went to the TV studios. She would have almost the whole day with me before taking the plane back to London, so we were planning to explore Dublin. Kathryn was almost as tired as I, so we quickly retreated to the room, planning on an early night, as we were being collected at 6:30 the next morning.

'Do you think you'll sleep, or are you nervous?'

'I'm fine; I'm so tired, I'm sure I'll sleep like a log.'

'Me too, see you in the morning.'

I turned over and was asleep within seconds.

'Are you awake?' I asked Kathryn as I got out of bed the next morning.

'Yes, I've been awake for a while.'

'I'll get into the shower quickly, then it's all yours. We won't have time for breakfast, but we can make tea or coffee.'

'Don't worry; I'm sure they'll give us something at the TV studio.'

Kathryn and I got ready, not talking much. We just carried on by ourselves. I opened the curtains. It was already light and the early morning traffic was starting to pick up outside. I watched people scurrying to the bus stop, rushing to catch the bus, which had just pulled up outside. I sighed as one old man missed the bus by the skin of his teeth, banging on the back window as it pulled out to rejoin the traffic. He walked slowly over to the seat in the bus shelter and took out a newspaper, holding it close to his face in order to read the fine print.

'I'm feeling nervous', Kathryn said.

'Why are you nervous? You'll just be watching!'

'I know, are you OK?'

'I'm fine; I'll just sit here and take a few deep breaths. Then I'll be ready to go.'

I had got into the swing of doing radio and TV interviews now. I would spend a few minutes of quiet time, say a quick prayer, tell myself I would be calm, and then try to think of it as just having a chat with friends. Imagining the number of people watching or listening would not help my nerves.

In a way, I was dreading the inevitable questions about my reaction to meeting John: how did I feel about it, how did I feel about him now? I didn't know. I knew I couldn't be with him ever again, but of course there was a connection. There always would be. It was pointless pre-empting what they might ask; honesty and spontaneity were the way to go.

There was one thing bugging me, though. I had always imagined John one day reading my book, but now I knew he may be watching or listening. In some ways what I said would be my message to him. I didn't want that to stand in the way of what I would say—I was not going to sugar-coat anything, but it was a little close to home. Many of the questions I had already been asked related to his family and the fact that they didn't give me his contact details. I couldn't lie about the hurt and pain this had caused me, but at the same time I had to be tactful, as the interview would have national coverage. *I'll cross that bridge later,* I thought to myself; *it's pointless worrying about it now.* Writing my book had never been about revenge. It was about the story itself, a question of giving the facts and allowing people to interpret them as they wanted.

The cab pulled up at the hotel entrance and a young driver with a broad Dublin accent asked: 'Are you Mary Monaghan for *AM Live?*'

'Yes, that's me.'

'OK, it will take us about twenty minutes, we have plenty of time.'

Kathryn and I sat in the back of the cab, checking out the Dublin traffic. It didn't take long before we'd pulled into an office complex and parked in front of the studio. A few minutes later we were led into a reception area.

'They will call you shortly for make-up', a young assistant said.

'Ooh, fancy!' Kathryn laughed.

'Yes, I didn't have that for the South African breakfast show; I went on as I was.'

I was called into the make-up room. Luckily they didn't plaster too much on my face, as I hate that heavily made-up feeling. I went back to join Kathryn.

'You don't look too different', she said.

'Thankfully not.'

'You'll be on after the ad break. I'll take you through in about five minutes', an officious young man with a clipboard said.

I was hoping I would have a chance to talk to the interviewers before we went live. I just had to tell them that I had seen John, it needed to be said. I was taken to the set and introduced to one of the presenters.

'Yours is a remarkable story', he said. 'I can't believe anyone could be so heartless.'

'You won't believe what happened on Saturday', I said.

I told him the story very quickly and as his co-presenter arrived he updated her. I could see the questions they were going to ask me already lined up on the autocue. They would have to ad lib this bit. They were dressed for summer: he was in an open-neck pale yellow shirt and she wore a soft pink summer dress. They both smiled at me encouragingly as we prepared for the interview.

I felt very comfortable as the interview began. The presenter started off saying that there had been a new development. So here I was, Mary Monaghan on Irish breakfast TV, breaking the news story that I had bumped into John! The interview went quickly. I felt at ease throughout. The news was out now, thank goodness. Liam could send out his press release and that would be that until *The Gerry Ryan Show* the next morning. Then I was home free.

Kathryn and I had come up with a plan for our day. First, we would meet our cousins Ellen and Pat O'Mahony at the hotel for coffee; then we'd have the day to ourselves to explore Dublin.

'It went well', Kathryn said when I eventually got back to the reception area. 'You were sandwiched between an ex-Miss Ireland launching her new Peaches and Cream underwear range and the first black Mayor of Portlaoise.'

'How about that?' I replied. 'Very good company!'

We found our cab and returned to the hotel.

'It'll be great to unwind', I said to Kathryn. 'The last few days have been such a whirlwind, so very intense, and no real time to gather my thoughts about what has happened.'

'You're right', she said. 'We can just potter around: see Grafton Street, go to Bewley's and Temple Bar. I also want to go to a music shop to look for a CD. Deirdre loves my Dolores Keane *Solid Ground*. I'm sure we'll find one somewhere.'

When we were on the bus, Liam phoned. 'There's been a lot of interest in the story. The *Sun* is trying to get someone out to Ballyshannon to get a photo of John. I've tried to phone his house for a comment, but there is no answer. You may get a call from the odd journalist wanting a comment from you, so keep your phone on.'

We got off the bus at Grafton Street. The weather wasn't the greatest, and it looked like rain.

'Maybe we should go into Bewley's for coffee', Kathryn said. 'That way we'll miss the rain. Besides, it's an institution—you have to go there.'

Bewley's had been in existence in Dublin for many years. It was a real old-fashioned coffee shop, on several levels, with dark wood furnishings and small tables. It was bustling with shoppers, tourists, and business-people. We made our way up rickety stairs to the second level and got a seat by the window overlooking the throng of shoppers below. Kathryn ordered tea and cheesecake and I ordered coffee and a scone. It was so nice to take a breather and slow down. The rain started to ease off and we popped into a home store to look for a wedding present for Nicola, my cousin Mary's daughter. Just at that moment, the phone rang. It was Paddy Clancy, a journalist from Donegal.

'Wasn't the meeting just a little too coincidental, a publicity stunt maybe?' he asked.

I was incensed. 'Do you think I'd have put myself through all that for publicity?' I retorted.

'Describe the meeting', he said.

I answered all Clancy's questions. I could tell he wanted to get an idea of the story from John's perspective too, but couldn't reach him. I didn't mind that he seemed anti-me. There are always two sides to every story. I don't think he or any other reporter did get hold of John, so his side of the story has never been told.

'Let's go', Kathryn said, and we headed down the road through the rain to a music shop, which she remembered as specialising in Irish music. The phone rang again: another journalist wanting me to answer some questions. I went outside to take the call, standing in the doorway to shelter from the rain, which was coming down in buckets.

'They're looking for a copy of the CD', Kathryn said when I finally went back inside. 'They have the cover but can't find the disc. Who was on the phone?'

'Another journalist, from the *Daily Express* this time.'

'Wow, it seems to be causing quite a stir!'

The phone rang again and I went back outside to take the call. Kathryn waited patiently inside but the shop owner had no luck tracing the CD. The rain continued to bucket down.

'Shall we head for Temple Bar?' Kathryn asked.

'Yes, let's do that. If we run over the road to the bus stop we can catch a bus there. Luckily, there's a bus shelter.'

Crossing the road, we got totally soaked. The rain just wasn't letting up. The phone rang yet again. I fielded the call: a radio station requesting an interview for the next day.

'Why don't we just head back to the hotel?' I said to Kathryn. 'It's pouring with rain, the phone doesn't stop ringing, and at least there we can kick off our shoes and relax. I'm beginning to feel frazzled. It'll also give me a chance to check my emails.'

'Are you sure you don't mind? You've never explored Dublin before and you still haven't seen anything.'

'Don't worry, Dublin will always be there and I need to keep myself reasonably rested. Tomorrow is also a big day for me.'

We hopped on the next bus to the hotel. It was a good decision. My phone kept ringing, but at least I could answer questions from the sanctuary of my hotel room and not on the streets where I was beginning to resemble a drowned rat. My feet were soaked, my shoes had not coped well with all the puddles, my hair was plastered to my face, my jacket was soaking. I started to shiver; I needed to get into warm, dry clothes. Eventually the calls stopped and Kathryn and I prepared for an early supper at Ellen and Pat's.

Liam phoned. 'How has it been? Has there been interest?'

'That's for sure, the phone hasn't stopped ringing.'

'Check the papers tomorrow morning', he said. 'You'll be in most of them, I'm sure.'

'I will. I'll take a look before I leave for *The Gerry Ryan Show.* Thanks for everything, Liam.'

'You're welcome. We'll chat again tomorrow.'

Kathryn and I went out for an early supper before she left to catch her return flight to London. Fortunately the phone calls had stopped and we could laugh and joke with Ellen and Pat about the hurly-burly day that had just been. I was looking forward to what tomorrow might bring.

Dublin 2007 — interview time

Chapter 13

Nowhere to Hide

People say you get over it.

The next morning I woke to the sound of my cell phone alarm. The bed-clothes were hardly rumpled; I had had a restful night, barely moving. I had slept well after my hectic day, which had started with breaking the news of seeing John on *AM Live*. It was still early by Irish standards—half past six—but I had decided on an early start so that I could catch the local newsagent to pick up the papers before breakfast. The hotel only received the *Irish Times* and the *Irish Independent*. I was sure that my story was more likely to be featured in the tabloids.

I decided to do my hair after my trip to the newsagent. *The Gerry Ryan Show* was at ten, so there was plenty of time. I walked out of the hotel lobby into the grey of a Dublin early morning. It was overcast but not too cold, and didn't seem to be threatening rain. A walk down the road would be a relaxing way to start the day. As I was on my way to the newsagent I received a message from Kathryn: *Anything in the papers?* She was just as curious as I was to see what was in them.

On my way to get them, I replied.

The newsagent was a good ten- to fifteen-minute walk away, down some residential streets away from the traffic. The residents were starting to prepare for work, putting their briefcases in the boot, loading children into the back seat. *There's the newsagent just up ahead.* People who read newspapers and magazines in shops generally irritated me, but I needed to page though these to check if the story featured. It most certainly did—in every single Irish national newspaper bar one, the *Irish Times*. Not only did it feature, but it was given prominence: at least half a page, if not a full page, in each, with my usual publicity photos for the book: snaps of John and me in Zimbabwe and one of our wedding day. I was getting tired of seeing those photos over and over again, but they were the ones I had provided and I had no others with me, so there was nothing I could do to add more variety.

I went to the till, balancing four copies of each newspaper. The people in the newsagent must have wondered what was going on. I couldn't wait to get back to the hotel to read the articles properly. I sent a quick SMS to Kathryn, as I wanted to catch her before she left for school. She was trying to get the local newsagent in Cricklewood, Eddie (a friend of ours from our 1980s Galtymore days), to hold copies of the papers for her.

I walked back to the hotel clutching the newspapers, trying to process what had happened in the last few days. It had been overwhelming, John appearing out of the blue and the public involvement in all this. What had always been such a private issue was now totally in the public eye. There was no way I could escape that. It was my choice to write my book and put my story out there, but I had no idea just how far-reaching the consequences would be. There was nothing I could do about it now, it was too late. I would just ride out the interviews and continue to be as honest as I possibly could be. The problem was that I kept being asked how I felt about meeting John, but in all honesty I wasn't sure, that was the truth. I was still trying to understand what had happened. It was all so sudden and I didn't know how to react to it. Time would probably give me a better perspective, but right now there was just no time.

Sitting on the bed with the pile of papers, I cast my eye over the articles. They covered the same basic facts, but all with slightly different angles. All were very sympathetic to

Irish Daily Mirror

me, thank goodness. Writing my book had exposed me to the scrutiny of readers and that had opened me to their feedback, positive or negative. I had been lucky so far: people had been totally supportive.

I was uncertain, though, how my interview with Gerry Ryan would go. I had heard about his reputation for being a tough interviewer and cutting straight to the chase. By all accounts he made it very clear if he liked or disliked you, so an interview with him could be a pleasant experience or a very uncomfortable one. *Let's hope it's the former,* I thought to myself. *I'm just going to be true to myself as my mother always taught me and respond with openness and honesty.*

I decided to take one of the newspapers downstairs with me when I went for breakfast. The dining room was a large, old-fashioned, wood-panelled room, with a breakfast buffet in the alcove. A good hearty breakfast would set me up for the day ahead, I thought to myself. Just my interview with Gerry Ryan and one more afterwards, and then I would be on my way back to London. I took full advantage of the breakfast buffet: black and white pudding and potato cakes. It would be a while before I got a chance to have them again.

I looked at a man sitting in the corner. He was reading the newspaper and glancing up at me from time to time. This continued for most of the time I was eating my breakfast. As I left the dining room I looked at his newspaper. It was open on the page with my story—he had recognised me. What a strange feeling that was, a complete stranger being privy to such personal details of my life.

I went up to the room with an hour to go before the car was due to collect me and take me to the studio. I jumped into the shower and washed my hair. Just as I was drying off I got a call from Midwest Radio: 'I'm calling from *The Tommy Marren Show.* Tommy wants to know if you could do an update for us. We see your meeting with John is all over the national newspapers. Could we call you in about ten minutes, please?'

'Could you rather make it twenty minutes please? I'll be ready then.'

'Yes, of course. We'll phone you on this number.'

I put the phone down; water had dripped all over the bed. So much for having ample time to get ready. I knew no one would see me when I was on the radio, but somehow I felt more confident if I was looking good. I rushed to get dressed and dry my hair before the telephone call.

'Hello, this is *The Tommy Marren Show*. Can we do the interview now, please?'

'Yes, that's fine.'

'This is Tommy Marren. I'm talking to Mary Monaghan, doing an exclusive interview for Midwest Radio before she appears on *The Gerry Ryan Show* later this morning. You heard it here first, folks! We didn't think when we spoke to Mary on Thursday that two days later she would bump into her husband, John! Tell us about it, Mary.'

And so I relayed the story of bumping into John in Ballyshannon. I was glad I had the chance to tell the story on Midwest first. It felt right somehow; Midwest was home for me. The interview finished and I continued to get ready for *The Gerry Ryan Show*. I felt calmer, as if this had been a preparation for what was to come. I checked my hair and my clothes and went down to the lobby. The car was already there: a black Mercedes. I hopped in the back clutching a bottle of water, a dry mouth always a sign of nerves. I took deep breaths. *The Gerry Ryan Show* was going to be a big hurdle; it wasn't going to follow the pattern of the other shows I had done. But it was going to be good. I knew that even if Gerry was difficult with me I would tell it like it was—that was the best I could do. I fidgeted from side to side in the back of the car, crossing and uncrossing my legs. I knew the anticipation was always the worst; once I got there and the interview started I would be fine.

We pulled up outside the RTE studios. I completed the security form at reception and waited to be collected. An assistant came to meet me and took me to the cafeteria, where we had coffee together. It was an open, airy place with drinks and snacks, and full of people. There were probably some well-known people sitting close by, but I didn't recognise any of them. The assistant explained that they were running late, as a major news story had broken that morning: a drugs bust off the coast of Cork. She would fetch me in another twenty minutes or so. That was fine; the show was piped through to the cafeteria so I could follow what was happening and prepare myself. Thank goodness for my bottle of water. I kept sipping away at it to calm my nerves. They went into an ad break and then the assistant came back to take me into the studio.

Gerry Ryan stood up to greet me—I recognised him instantly from his pictures on the RTE website. He had dark hair, a light pink shirt, and a warm handshake. He was friendly, smiling broadly at me. We chatted before going on air. 'It's an extraordinary story', he said. 'I started thinking you must be mad, but eventually I got to understand you. My wife and I discussed it last night. OK, we're on now.'

Gerry asked me many probing questions—he was obviously intrigued with my story.

He might be psychiatrically ill, that's one possibility?
What about John's mother?
Did you want him back?
How do you feel about it now: is it all gone, exorcised?
How can he move on if he doesn't live up and own up?

I was conscious that both John and his mother and many other members of his family would be listening. This would be my opportunity to send them any messages I might want to, but I was also conscious that this show had a large listenership and, despite John's betrayal—and to a lesser extent, that of his mother—I didn't want to be bitter and trash them. This was never what it was about. I was mindful of this in my responses.

The interview flew by. I was on for over forty minutes, which was apparently very good, as Gerry could cut short interviews if he became bored with the topic. He was very complimentary about my book, calling it "a small book with a big story, an amazing story, fantastically well told". We finished off, he shook my hand and thanked me, and off I went back to the hotel.

I planned to change into more comfortable clothes and spend a little time on the phone trying to sort out printers and distributors in Ireland. I turned the radio on and then immediately turned it off again. I didn't want any noise, as my head was full enough without adding any external noise to it. I paced around the room for a few minutes, trying to settle myself again. I consciously slowed my breathing, closed my eyes, and pictured the view from my house in Grotto Bay: the waves on the rocks, Dassen Island in the distance. I immediately felt calmer.

I put on some jeans and a light sweatshirt, then settled in to look up the phone numbers I needed. It was extraordinary—both printers and book distributors had been unresponsive to my queries before; now, all of sudden, their attitude had changed. Now that my story had been splashed all over the newspapers and I had been on *The Gerry Ryan Show*, doors had started to open to me. Both Easons and Argosy now wanted to order. Luckily, I had managed to find a printer who was willing to do a rush print job for me.

What a turnaround, and all because of meeting John! Ironically, he had finally done me a favour by showing up—inadvertently so, but a favour nonetheless. I tried to decide whether I would rather not have bumped into him on that day in Ballyshannon, but figured it was meant to be; it needed to happen and the timing was right. Yes, it had knocked me off balance, but I had always known it would. I had known that inevitably one day our paths would probably cross, much as I had been trying to convince myself I was unlikely to ever see him again. At least it had happened now and I had survived, so it would no longer be something that was hanging over me. I would have time to think things over more slowly and carefully when I was back in South Africa. Now all that remained was for me to make sense of it all.

I packed my case and prepared to leave for the airport. I had planned to take the airport shuttle bus but after the drama of the last few days I felt I deserved a taxi. After arranging for a cab to pick me up, I took the lift downstairs. I loaded my luggage into the taxi, sat back, and decided to drink in the sights and sounds of Dublin. I had intended to see so much of it, but I hadn't had a chance. *Next time,* I thought to myself. The taxi driver had other plans for me, however. He was talkative, and wanted to know about my trip to Dublin. I didn't intend to mention the radio interview but two sentences into our conversation he recognised my voice.

'You're the one that was interviewed on *The Gerry Ryan Show*—what a story!'

The taxi driver then proceeded to give me his views on what had happened. Like everyone else I had talked to, he was very kind.

My phone rang: a request for another radio interview. I would be at the airport then, I explained, probably in the departure lounge. They thought it would be quiet enough there, so we set a time. Luckily I was due to arrive at the airport early, so as to have time to shop. I hadn't bought a thing on my trip and with my black belt in shopping that was a poor performance—there had just been no time.

The driver dropped me at Departures. My heart sank as I approached the check-in counters. The queue stretched forever. Not only were check-in procedures lengthy, but the trip through security was equally bad. I glanced at my watch: five minutes to go before the interview. I went into a restaurant area and found a relatively secluded spot. I tried to remain shielded from the hustle and bustle of the departure lounge as the interviewer spoke to me. I crossed my fingers that no announcements would be made over the PA system. I tried to talk as quietly as possible but the interviewer asked me to speak up. I did so and saw a couple of passersby raise their eyebrows and give me reproving looks, muttering at my lack of cell phone etiquette in a public place.

The interview went well, but I felt all too keenly how incongruous it was to be relaying such a personal story at the top of my voice in public. I'd have to hurry up, or I'd miss my flight. I trotted off to the departure gate and made the plane with five minutes to spare. This trip was bringing new meaning to the term *whistle-stop*.

One day left in London—a night at the Pink Rupee. How could I miss catching up with everyone? It was such a tradition.

Kathryn and I made our way down the road to the Pink Rupee, which was just a few blocks away from her flat. It was warm and humid in London and I could feel my top sticking to my back. The owners greeted Kathryn warmly and showed us to our usual table. She was a regular there, as was I on all my trips to London. There were going to be about twelve of us. They had all been following the saga of my meeting with John and were excited to get the inside track on all the events in Ireland.

The table filled up and we ordered an array of delicious Indian dishes, changing seats constantly so that we could all get a chance to talk to each other. Our usual table had a commanding view of the restaurant. It was busy, people coming in and out, some for takeaways, some to enjoy a meal there. Pictures of Nepal adorned the walls; it was all so pleasantly familiar. Enjoying the noisy, vibrant atmosphere, we toasted life and new beginnings with Cobra beer and red wine. This too was a coming home for me.

The next day I was due to fly back to Cape Town. Kathryn would take me to the airport after school. She had been running around so much for me, and we had hardly had any time together. I hope she realised just how much I appreciated all her help and support.

Before leaving, I popped in to see the nuns next door to the school in Hampstead where Kathryn now taught. I met with Sister Dominica, my ex-headmistress and English teacher. She no longer wore the veil or habit I remembered her in as a schoolgirl. I found it hard to relate to her with her head uncovered, her face no longer framed by her veil. When she smiled at me and spoke to me I remembered her vividly, standing in front of the class, patiently guiding us through the complexities of Shakespeare's sonnets. How daunting to meet her when I had now written a book! I still felt like a small child in her presence, especially as I recalled her marking my English compositions. Goodness knows what she had thought of *Remember Me?* But far from giving a critique of my book, she was just interested in all the gossip around my meeting John. Life definitely moves on.

By the time I had got to Heathrow, checked in my suitcase, and gone through two security checks, I had no energy left to shop. I was exhausted. I slept like a baby and landed back at Cape Town, where I filled in the customs declaration form: not one single item to declare, not even a book or a CD. I pushed my trolley out of Arrivals, to be met by Diane. Now the time had come to share my story with my South African friends.

Chapter 14

Brief Encounter

Always be true to yourselves.

Everyone so wanted me to find a good man. I was always asked in my interviews about having a man in my life; it came up again and again.

And what about relationships since John? Has it put you off men?

Being asked this question time and time again, I reflected on the men who had been in my life since John had gone away. I was determined not to let my experience with John taint any future relationships. I was open to meeting someone if the time was right, but I wasn't looking for just anyone. I knew that my friends so wanted me to have someone in my life; and if truth were told, I probably did too, but not for the sake of it. I knew that I didn't need a Prince Charming to feel alive and fulfilled. If a wonderful man came along that would be fun, but my life was plenty full enough without one.

I had not had a serious boyfriend before I had met John, never getting involved in the dating game while I was studying. It was a scary world for me once I became single again. I had started to think of myself as being single after the annulment obtained through the Catholic Church in 1997 and was then open to start meeting new people. It had been a difficult and unsettling period for me, trying to find my way. I had not found Mr.

Right but I had some interesting moments along the way: my time with Juan and my relationship with Michael. This was followed a few years later by an attempt at an Internet romance.

It was an early autumn day in May 2006 when my Irish friend Ann and I set off for a hike in Noordhoek, a beautiful part of the Cape.

'Hi Mary, are you ready for the hike?' Ann asked.

'Oh yes, I can't wait, some fresh air is just what I need.'

I had known Ann for several years since 1995, when she and Neville, her husband, had moved to the Cape at just the same time as I started visiting Cape Town regularly with my new job at Gilbey's. We met each time I visited and became good friends.

Since I had moved to Cape Town permanently in 2000, we tried to get out as much as possible. This wasn't easy, as Ann had twins, Niamh and Jamie, and it was hard to fit in time for herself in between her family commitments. But now she had finally managed some time out. A break would be good for me too, as I was in the process of editing my book and was finding it tough going.

It was a perfect day for our walk, not too hot as autumn was approaching. There was very little wind, hardly a cloud in the sky. We had planned a two- to three-hour walk along the beach at Noordhoek; it promised to be a joy for the soul.

'How are things going?' asked Ann.

'Well', I replied, 'heavy going with the editing, but I am making progress. I can't believe that this book may soon actually be out there, it's a scary thought.'

'It's what you want, though.'

'Oh yes, it just exposes so much personal stuff. It's what I want, but it makes me feel quite exposed at the same time.'

'Yes, I can imagine.'

Ann and I always had a lot to talk about: personal things, politics, and books we had read. I related well to Ann on so many levels, and it was always good to speak to someone who came from the same Irish background as I, it made it so easy to relate to each other. As the walk progressed I felt the need to share something with Ann, which I hadn't told another soul. She was open and non-judgemental; I knew I could share my secret with her.

'You probably won't believe this, but I tried my hand at Internet dating in a moment of boredom.'

'You did?'

'I know, I can't believe I did it either! I have met someone who seems such a good match. It's been three years since Michael; it's about time I tried again.'

I started to tell Ann about Robert: based in Los Angeles, a history teacher, about my age; we had started corresponding a few weeks earlier and had become friendly. We talked about music, art, literature, and life in our different parts of the world. He was very well read and cultured, and my interaction with him was intellectually stimulating, something so important for me in a man.

Ann was intrigued. 'Hold on, let's stop here for a while. Let's grab some water. Here's a good spot, sit down, slow down, and tell me all.' We sat on a rock, the light breeze helping to cool us down. The tide was low and the sea was far away in the distance. Many riders were taking the opportunity to ride their horses along the beach. I leant against the rock, and continued my story.

I told Ann that Robert and I had exchanged photos. He was tall, good-looking, quite the catch. I explained to her how strange I found it, having very deep and personal conversations with someone I had never met.

'Enjoy it for what it is', she advised. 'It must be quite something to converse on that kind of level.'

'Yes it is, we do it via MSN Chat. The only problem is that with the time difference, we often do it early in the morning my time, which can be a killer.'

'I'm sure you'll manage it.'

I fully intended to see where this online relationship would go. I was no longer working nine to five now that I had left my job to finish my book, so I had time to devote to emailing and chatting with Robert. It was a welcome diversion. Besides, it couldn't go anywhere, as we were worlds apart.

Robert was old-fashioned, in a way. He wrote beautifully, something that was also very important for me. He loved the idea of chivalry and honour, which did appeal to me after my experience with John. How perfect it would be to be involved with someone with old-fashioned values for a change!

Eventually we spoke. Robert had a soft American accent. I was finding myself becoming more and more attracted to him. He told me he was an only child. His father had died when he was young but he still spent a lot of time with his aged mother. He was religious, attending a Methodist church each Sunday. I told him about myself, my background, and my experience with John. Opening up to Robert felt comfortable. His mother was of French descent so we had our interest in things French in common, too. Imagine the excitement when we discovered we both had already planned trips to Paris at exactly the same time in July 2006! I was beginning to believe more and more that fate had intervened. We were destined to meet.

This was becoming so exciting. I had planned a few days in Paris as usual to visit my school friend Ruth, and also take in the museums and galleries. Robert would be there with his mother; they had a small apartment close to the hotel where I usually stayed.

We decided it would be best to meet at a small café near the river, somewhere public and relaxed; but as the time of the meeting approached Robert suggested he should meet me at the Gare du Nord, where I was due to arrive on the Eurostar train. That made sense to me, especially as I was never the best at travelling light; any help with my luggage would be gratefully received.

Robert was due to arrive in Paris before I was. He would email from there, as I would be able to pick up mail from my sister Kathryn's flat in London where I would be spending a few days. I decided to tell Kathryn my plan. She was a little concerned about me meeting a total stranger in Paris, but I reassured her that I had taken all the necessary precautions; and anyway, he sounded very genuine so I didn't anticipate any problems.

The day before I left London I picked up a mail from Robert saying how much he was looking forward to seeing me; but if for any reason he did not make it to the Gare du Nord, to please proceed to the hotel and he would contact me there. I found this strange given his impatience to meet me, but quickly put any concerns out of my mind as I prepared to meet friends and family for dinner at the Pink Rupee.

The next morning I said goodbye to Kathryn and left for my adventure. A rendezvous in Paris, it sounded so romantic. I had to catch the train at Waterloo Station. It was peak holiday season, so the queues to go through security seemed endless. Luckily, I had left plenty of time (as usual), so wasn't worried about being late.

I boarded the train with time to spare and took my book out of my bag. Any thoughts of spending the journey reading were soon gone. My mind was racing with thoughts of Robert. Would he be at the station? Would he look like his photo? What if we didn't get on in real life? I soon put the book away, kicked off my shoes, and gazed out of the window, trying to calm myself by giving myself over to the rhythmic movement of the train. I glanced at my watch; only ten minutes had passed since I had previously checked it. *Get a grip,* I thought to myself, *at this stage you will arrive looking like a nervous wreck!*

Finally the train pulled into the station. I had spent the last ten minutes checking my hair, fixing my lipstick, just hoping that Robert would be there but working on Plan B should this not be the case.

I stepped off the train, lugging my red bag behind me; I scanned the faces of the people waiting to greet the new arrivals, looking for someone vaguely familiar. No one. *So much for the romantic meeting on the platform,* I thought to myself. I waited another five minutes just to be sure that he hadn't arrived, and then made my way to the Metro. I scrabbled in my purse for euros to buy a carnet of tickets whilst holding on to my case and handbag; travelling alone and having to keep track of your entire luggage is always such a pain. I was starting to feel hot and bothered; Paris in July was hot and sticky. I could feel my clothes starting to stick to me. So much for first impressions.

Luckily, the Metro station was very close to the hotel. I was oh so glad to open the door to the air-conditioned reception and breathe in the cool air. The receptionist greeted me warmly. 'Your friend Monsieur Robert has been here, he is just busy doing some laundry down the road, and he will call back in about half an hour.'

I thanked her and made my way to the room. That gave me enough time to shower and change before meeting Robert. But what on earth did she mean about the laundry? Maybe my rusty French had caused me to misunderstand. Surely I hadn't been stood up at the station because Robert was busy with his laundry?

I felt so much better after my shower, far more human and ready to meet Robert for the first time. I was busy unpacking my case when the phone rang; it was Robert. 'Welcome to Paris, my dear, I'm sorry I couldn't make it to the station.'

'Don't worry, I'll be down in a few minutes', I replied. I put on my shoes, brushed my hair, and took the small lift down to the reception. There he was. He seemed shorter than in the photo. Despite the intense heat of the day, he was wearing a tweed jacket that had seen better days, with a blue shirt and blue tie. Not quite what I had expected, but then again dress sense isn't everything. Robert shook my hand and suggested we go for coffee. We went to a little café over the road. He looked hot and bothered and asked if I minded if he took his jacket off. Not at all, as it looked very incongruous in this heat. I now discovered his shirt was of the blue short-sleeved variety; there was definitely work needed here. Our conversation had flowed so freely over the Internet and by phone, but in person it was stilted and disjointed. *Give it time,* I thought to myself.

Robert kept glancing at his watch. 'I'm sorry, my dear, I have to go back to the laundromat in ten minutes to take the clothes out of the dryer.' Now here was a first—I honestly was playing second fiddle to his laundry! 'I won't be long, I'll be back in a few minutes', and with that, he went off down the road.

I smiled ruefully, battling to relate the previous scene to Robert's talk of chivalry, nobility, and romantic love. This was definitely not going the way I had imagined. There was a massive disconnect between the romance of our Internet relationship and the mundanity of our first meeting. I decided to give him the benefit of the doubt. It was early days; I shouldn't rush to hasty conclusions. However, there were alarm bells sounding in my head.

Robert arrived back about ten minutes later, sweating profusely, profoundly apologetic. He reached over to hold my hand. 'I am so sorry, my dear; I will make it up to you.'

'Yes, we have so many days ahead of us to visit Paris, the galleries, the museums ... '

He looked sheepish, staring at the empty cup in front of him.

'There has been an unexpected development, my dear. My mother has been invited to a family gathering in Italy and she can't fly alone, so I am accompanying her. We leave tomorrow. It is only for a few days, I will be back before you leave.'

I was lost for words. I had come to Paris expecting to meet the man who had been wooing me, but first I was stood up at the station, then I was stood up for some laundry, and now this "unexpected" trip to Italy. I looked at Robert coolly. 'You must do what you have to do', I said.

'I'll email you from Italy and we can go for long walks along the Seine when I come back.'

'We'll see', I replied.

'I'm sorry I must go now, but I will see you in a few days. You are everything I ever dreamed of.'

And with that, he put his tweed jacket back on and walked down the street. I was at a loss to understand what had just happened. It seemed that Robert thought it was acceptable to treat me in this way, and expected me to wait patiently for his return. I couldn't match the romantic writing of his emails with the reality of meeting him. In his mind, at least, all was fine, that was the way things were.

I gathered up my things and walked back to the hotel, bumping into people on the busy sidewalks, not paying attention to where I was going. I had too much on my mind. I felt claustrophobic, I needed air, the tall city buildings were closing in on me. What a disappointment, no Prince Charming for me. I tried to work out if there had been warning signs, but there had been nothing until Robert said he may not be able to meet me at the station. It seemed like he lived in a fantasy world that bore no resemblance to reality.

I vowed not to let this impinge on my enjoyment of Paris. I was more than capable of enjoying it on my own as I had initially planned to; it just would have been nice to share the experience with someone special for a change. I put Robert out of my mind, met up with Ruth and her family, and did my rituals of going to the Musee d'Orsay, the Louvre, and Tuileries Gardens; walking along the Seine and having coffee at Les Deux Magots. I then discovered the Jeu de Paume for the first time. Calmed by the beauty of the Monet Water Lilies displayed in the round, I sat in the cool air-conditioned room on one of the benches, taking in the colours and texture. To be surrounded by such beauty spoke to my soul. I blocked out the noise of the tourists strolling in and out of the room and let the pale pinks, lilacs, and blues of the painting colour my thoughts.

I sent a short text message to those friends in whom I had confided about my first meeting with Robert, to tell them that it hadn't worked out but not to worry, as I was having a ball in Paris. I had now done everything I had wanted to and decided there was no point in waiting for Robert's return. What purpose would it serve? I didn't want to see him again. There was no place in my life for someone who treated me so disrespectfully, I deserved better. I changed my Eurostar ticket to an earlier date, sent Robert an email to say I was returning to London and why and headed off to the Gare du Nord.

How different this journey was; yet again, I couldn't settle to read my book, but this time because my head was full of what had happened. I felt proud of myself, not hanging around meekly for Robert's return. No one would get away with treating me like that; I had become a much stronger and more independent person than the one John had left behind all those years ago.

I knew my friends would be sad for me, but it hadn't been all bad. The end result had been disappointing, but leading up to it there had been a few months when I had floated around, enjoying the romance of it all, feeling loved and cherished, and nothing could take that away. I didn't need a man in my life right now, especially one that wasn't right for me. I had more than enough to keep me busy, considering it was only a few months before my book would be published.

I had indeed had other relationships since John, some better than others. The good thing was that I knew John had not put me off men for life. I was certainly more wary than before, but I remained a romantic at heart, never discounting the fact that there could be a wonderful man out there who would be perfect for me. I deserved a special man, but if there wasn't one for me it was OK. I was doing so many things and had such great friends, what more could I possibly need?

Family gathering in London

Chapter 15

And Now for Something Completely Different

I met a lot of different nationalities.

I suppose the question remained: *Where to now?* I had written my book, which had led to an unexpected encounter with John. Meeting John had been a good thing; it laid to rest many demons. But I still needed to sort out fully in my own mind what my reaction to finding him was. To come face to face with someone who had caused such pain was shattering. The worst was probably that in so many ways I felt sorry for him, while at the same time berating myself for making such a big deal out of it all for so many years. That in itself was devastating: realising how many good years of my life had been wasted, waiting and searching for someone who at the end of the day probably wasn't worth it.

It was a cold and wet winter's day in Grotto Bay in June 2007 when I rushed to answer my cell phone.

'Hi Mary, can you talk now? It's Werner speaking.'

'I can, but it needs to be quick. I am just about to go into the bank to pick up my foreign exchange.'

'Oh, I see. Where are you off to?'

'Ireland. I am going over there to do some radio and TV interviews and a book signing.'

'Wow, that's great! You didn't tell me about that when we spoke a few weeks ago.'

'That's because I didn't know, this has come up unexpectedly in the last few days.'

I explained about the publicity that had just happened around my book in Ireland and my last-minute decision to go over there.

I had known Werner since he was a change consultant at Guinness UDV. At that stage he was working for Deloitte Consulting. Werner and I worked closely together and had become friends. He was based in Pretoria, so we only saw each other rarely, but he kept in touch and never forgot to phone me on my birthday. Werner had set up a change management consultancy with some other partners and would phone me now and again to see if I was available to do some work for them.

'Are you still working on the HIV project with Diane?' he asked.

'Yes, we've almost finished all the translations as well as the shooting of the DVD.'

'When will you be finishing up?'

'I'm not quite sure.'

'OK, I'll be in touch when you get back. Send us an updated CV so we have something on hand if an interesting project comes up.'

'I'll contact you when I get back, I'll have more time to chat then.'

I had been overseeing the translation of an HIV and Aids toolkit into five South African official languages. It was an amazing project, and I knew it would help people understand the nature of the disease and the importance of knowing their status. It was something I was passionate about, I knew it could help to make a difference. Now that the project was nearing completion, my time of working with Diane was drawing to a close.

I resolved to phone Werner as soon as I got back from Ireland. Little did I know then the impact that my trip to Ireland would have and the events it would trigger. As it turned out, it took me a few weeks after my return to phone him.

'Wow!' Werner said, excited at my news. 'No wonder you have taken your time to get back to me! I'll send the templates and then you need to format your CV. I'll have it on file then, and I'll let you know if anything comes up.'

I received the templates the next day, completed them, and sent them back to Werner.

I was gradually getting back into my routine after all the excitement of my Ireland trip when I got a call from Werner.

'Hi there, do you speak French?' he asked.

'Yes I do, French and Spanish, that was my degree.'

'There is a possibility of a contract coming up in Mauritius for a few months, would you be interested?'

'Oh, yes!' I replied.

I didn't have to think twice; Mauritius seemed much more interesting than a project based in Kimberley or Rustenburg, the opportunities Werner had spoken to me about previously.

'I'll find out some more about it and I'll get back to you, probably by tomorrow.'

I put the phone down, thinking how lucky I was to be so mobile and to make my decision immediately without having to consult anyone. A project in Mauritius sounded like such an adventure. I waited impatiently for Werner's next phone call.

'Mary, I'm sorry', he said, 'I knew the name of the country began with an 'M' but it is Madagascar, not Mauritius. I got mixed up.'

'No problem', I replied. Both of them sounded exotic to me. I loved to travel, and time on an Indian Ocean island would be just up my street.

Werner took me through the details of the project, an eight-month contract as a transition support consultant for a division of the international mining and resources group Rio Tinto. Initially I would be based in the capital, Antananarivo, then move down to the coast to Fort Dauphin/ Tolagnaro. He explained that it was for a mining operation currently in a construction phase. There was a computer implementation happening and they needed a consultant to cover change management and training. The mine was similar to one in operation in Richards Bay and the team managing the implementation was based in Brisbane, Australia. How about that? A double whammy, the two places I had a thing about because of John, now coming back to haunt me! I was definitely being asked to confront my demons.

Werner said I would receive a call from Anita Jordaan from Rio Tinto Johannesburg to do a telephonic interview, and then if it went well, I would be interviewed by her boss in Brisbane. I was excited, it sounded like an opportunity and a real challenge. I was definitely ready for that.

The next day Anita phoned to interview me. I sat at my desk in Grotto Bay, looking out to sea, and answered her questions as best I could. We laughed when I recounted my experiences of visiting the gorillas in Uganda. I could tell she was concerned whether I would be able to handle the basic environment in Madagascar. Hearing that I had travelled extensively in Africa allayed her fears.

Anita told me Michelle Bourke, her boss, would arrange to phone me from Brisbane. I waited impatiently to hear from her. The more I thought about it, the more this seemed like a great opportunity. Anita had explained that, from a social perspective, there was very little to do in Madagascar; but that would suit me just fine. I would have no distractions and could get on with writing my screenplay. So many people had said that my book would make a great film; my friend Liam O'Brien had given me some pointers on how to do it. I just needed some time to get it finished, and what better place than Madagascar for that?

Days turned into weeks—no more contact from Rio Tinto. I resigned myself to the fact that it wasn't going to happen when I got a call out of the blue from Werner. Michelle would call me the next day. She phoned me early the next morning and we had a brief chat, mostly exploring my adaptability to working under difficult conditions and having various reporting lines. I chatted easily to her and felt it went well. Now I would just have to wait and see.

The next day Anita called: they wanted me to start as soon as possible. I explained that my cousin Mary had planned a trip from Ireland to visit me, so I had to be there for her before I set off for Madagascar. I agreed with Anita that I would go to Johannesburg for a few days' induction and briefing, then spend some days with Mary before leaving for Madagascar. Everything was coming together. I arranged my trip to Johannesburg for the following week: the start of another new adventure, new beginnings once again.

Everything had happened so quickly. I was excited at the idea of the project, and also Madagascar sounded so exotic. I was well aware that it was still very third world, and that staying there was going to be an experience, but a challenge never frightened me. I had closed the chapter on

John and a new chapter was opening.

Anita was a bubbly, warm, dark-haired woman, very welcoming. There was a lot of information I needed to sift through concerning the Rio Tinto approach and methodology I would be required to implement. My head was buzzing by the end of the first day. I could see that the project was going to be both very challenging and stimulating at the same time.

The second day at Rio Tinto proved just as information-full as the first. My head was reeling after looking at presentations, spreadsheets, reports. It was daunting. I went to the kitchen to make some coffee and hurried back as I heard my cell phone ring. We were in a large open plan office, so it was frowned on to let it ring for too long. The ID showed a private number: probably somebody trying to sell me something, I thought to myself. No it wasn't—it was John.

Of all the days for him to phone, he chose now, when I was in an unfamiliar environment, an open plan office with next to no privacy, and at a time when I needed to maintain my composure and my air of professionalism. My hand shook as I held the phone to my ear, almost tripping over my feet as I rushed to get to a more private area.

'I said I would be in touch', John said.

'Yes you did', I replied.

He had indeed said he would when we met in Ballyshannon, but I had taken that promise with a pinch of salt, as there had been so many other broken promises along the way. John sounded pleased that he had done what he said he would do; I didn't know what to say to him. He had caught me by surprise and I couldn't talk to him. I stumbled over my words, caught off guard. I sat down carefully on one of the chairs. My legs were shaky and I felt unsteady on my feet. The drywall of the office was thin; I could hear murmurs from a meeting next door. I spoke to John in the darkness, not putting on the light, feeling that the dimness might calm me. I explained where I was and that I was starting a new project, going to Madagascar. He sounded very impressed.

'You are certainly a globetrotter', John said. I sensed a certain sarcasm in his voice and almost resentment of the fact that I had made something of my life without any help from him.

'I think about you often', he said. 'I will always love you.'

I gulped. 'I will always love you too', I replied. I was shocked at my response but it was true, part of me would always love him despite everything that had happened. At the same time there was no going back, I was a different person now and he no longer had a place in my life.

As we chatted a little more, John took the opportunity to express his sorrow at the hurt he had caused me. I couldn't help feeling that the phone call was done more as a means for him to make peace with what he had done than from any real desire to talk to me. It felt to me that once John had followed through on his promise to contact me again, he would be able to resume his life with a clearer conscience.

Having this conversation in these surroundings was a very uncomfortable experience for me; I was emotional and knocked off balance, and wanted to be sure that this didn't manifest itself to my new colleagues. The call came to an end at last, and we said we would be in touch again. I sat down at a desk far from everyone else, dabbing at my eyes and trying to take deep breaths to compose myself. I hated the fact that John could still have this effect on me. I had moved on with my life, and it was a great life, so why was I reacting like this? I felt vulnerable again as all the old pain and hurt resurfaced. That was it, I realised: talking to John brought back those memories, that was all. I felt in so many ways that I was talking to a stranger, but a stranger who had the ability to knock me off balance emotionally. I vowed to make sure that this would be the last time that John would have this effect on me.

I moved back into the office, a smile on my face, and settled at my desk looking intently at the computer screen. But all I could see was a blur in front of me as I tried to settle my thoughts. My stomach was unsettled, a common reaction when I was stressed, so I spent most of the rest of the day making frequent trips to the Ladies. I was sure the others in the office were wondering what was going on. I only wish I knew just what was going on, myself; all I could be sure of was that I had to deal with it and move on.

And at least moving on was in the cards. Working in Madagascar was a form of escapism, I suppose,

Madagascar

but it was probably also a time to reinvent myself. I knew I didn't need John any more, he was part of my past. Now I was definitely moving into a new life. I would make sure that this would be a time to look to the future without any baggage.

Roll on Madagascar and the new experiences it would bring!

Chapter 16

A New Life Begins

Green are the hills far away.

Fort Dauphin

Within the undivided moments
A palm tree rustles in the wind
And a mother holds her child to her breast
As a cart of meat buzzing with flies trundles by

Within the undivided moments
Seeds drop lightly on the lush grass
As a child cries with hunger
And a fishing boat goes out on the lake

Within the undivided moments
A flower sways in the breeze
And a mosquito lands on a child's face
As a family eats its daily meal of rice

Within the undivided moments
Clouds roll by driven by the wind
A man shivers with fever
As his son goes down to the river for water
Within the undivided moments

Mary Monaghan – Madagascar 2008

Standing at Johannesburg's O.R. Tambo Airport with Anita, checking in for our flight to Antananarivo, I was a little apprehensive. I didn't know quite what to expect. It was going to be so different: new people, a new environment. It was just what I needed, I was craving some time out, quiet time, time to reflect on how I felt about meeting John, time to move on again.

I needn't have been apprehensive. The rest of the project team were welcoming. Most of the consultants were from Mauritius, barring two from South Africa—myself and Jan Myburg, a taciturn Afrikaner who didn't speak French and had an aversion to "foreign food". Jan survived most of the time on fish and chips, turning his nose up at any remotely spicy food. We worked closely with our team from Rio Tinto, mostly French-speaking Canadians (Quebecois), and local Madagascans. They were all very welcoming, warming to me after their initial concern that I would be English speaking. Once they realised that I could speak French, albeit with an English accent, they relaxed.

We were based at the Sunny Hotel; we had big rooms and beds surrounded by mosquito nets, as malaria was an ever-present concern here. The hotel had a twenty-five-metre pool and a small gym, so I was glad to see that I could keep up with my exercise regime.

Lines of communication were difficult from a physical, phone, and email perspective. Power failures were a fairly standard occurrence, and the English/French language issues between ourselves and the teams in Johannesburg and Brisbane added to the mix.

Our project was due to come onstream, "go live", at the same time as in Namibia, parts of the U.S., and Australia. But these were all existing functioning sites, unlike ours, which was a "greenfields" site with many unknowns and intangibles. This was the cause of frustration initially, as the Australian team was putting a lot of demands on us, not realising the basic problems we were experiencing with connectivity, information, infrastructure. Little by little they started to understand the constraints, helped by the fact that some of their team had been to visit us and experienced life in Madagascar first-hand.

Tana, as the capital was commonly called, was a bustling city, jampacked with cars imported from Europe. It was like being in a time warp—old, totally ramshackle 2CVs, Renaults, Citroëns, mostly from the '70s and '80s, negotiating narrow, potholed, hilly streets, constantly sounding their hooters to indicate that they were turning, stopping ... in short, doing exactly what they felt like doing. The streets varied from muddy to dusty, depending on the rain. Sanitation was often a problem.

As you drove from the airport, you were greeted by rice paddies on one side of the road and previously beautiful houses, now almost ruins, on the other. Most places had seen better days—shutters falling off hinges, peeling paint, holes in the roof. This was one of the truly poorest countries in the world. On the way to the hotel we passed open stalls selling bread, cakes, appliances, clothes, and meat. Flies swarmed around meat that hung uncovered in the heat of the day at the butchers' stalls. Definitely a strong stomach was going to be required for this, I thought to myself. I became accustomed to eating in a very few select places, meticulously avoiding salads and ice cubes in my drink. I had heard horror stories of how sick you could get and wanted to avoid this at all costs.

Life settled into a routine of working hard, retreating to my room after supper, watching some TV, reading or writing and then going to bed and repeating the same the next day. I was lucky that I embraced the quiet time and used it to my advantage, but I could imagine how desperately boring life could be if you had no particular interests to keep you busy. It was an opportunity for me to focus on my screenplay.

Thank goodness for Liam, who patiently guided me through the process. I looked forward to our regular Skype calls, in which we discussed my progress. We were worlds apart: Liam an academic in a first-world environment, and me in a chaotic third-world one. Yet we connected through our creativity as we debated plot and character development. I could just visualise him sitting in his study, surrounded by books, looking out at the snow falling on the trees whilst I sat in the lobby of the hotel, speaking softly into my headset, crossing my fingers that the electricity would not fail, my body glistening with perspiration from the humidity as I listened to the buzzing of mosquitoes.

On Sundays a driver would take me to a Catholic church nearby for Mass. As consultants we weren't allowed to drive in Madagascar. It was considered too dangerous, which was probably true as driving techniques there were certainly different. It was the highlight of my week. I went to 8:30 AM Mass, as it was in French as opposed to Malagasy. The church was packed, full of people in their Sunday best. What I loved most of all was the fervour and spirit with which everyone participated, singing the hymns at the top of their voices. It was truly uplifting, and far removed from the genteel mumbling that so often accompanied the services I attended in South Africa. There was a joy and spirit that went right to your soul. Most of the congregation had so little, but they still found such joy. Living in Madagascar made me understand how little you actually need to get by, and that material things are so insignificant.

Madagascar transport

I had been there a few weeks when Jan Myburg asked me if I wanted to join him for a drive out of town on Saturday. Jan was a loner, and he generally kept to himself. He was a man of few words, and I'm sure my talkativeness irritated him, but I was the only other English-speaking person in the team, so we did spend some time together. I thought it sounded like an opportunity to explore, so I gladly accepted.

The driver picked us up at nine o'clock, and we drove out of town. This took some time, as we hit peak Saturday morning rush hour: cars, cattle pulling carts, people wandering onto the road, horns blaring at them to get out of the way. It was noisy and chaotic. As time went on I started to realise that Jan had an ulterior motive in asking me to accompany him: I was the interpreter, tasked with asking the driver all manner of questions as we drove along. Jan was very analytical, and this came through strongly in the very detailed and probing questions he asked. *Where does the piped water come from? What is the yield from the rice paddies? How much rice needs to be imported?* We visited some old palaces, wooden structures full of Victorian-era artefacts. When we stopped off for lunch, Jan stuck to his usual fish and chips, and I was more adventurous. We didn't spend too much time over lunch, as we were anxious to move on and explore further.

About ten minutes after leaving the restaurant we heard the sound of drums, singing, and chanting in the distance and quickly came upon a large group of people in a procession coming towards us. They were carrying something wrapped in straw on their shoulders and suddenly I realised that these were bodies exhumed from their tombs in a traditional ceremony. They were wrapped in shrouds and straw matting, brought out of their tombs to be honoured for the day. There were at least fifty people in the procession, dressed in their very best clothes, many of the women wearing hats to shield themselves from the strong sun. Their singing was joyful and they moved easily to the rhythm of the drums. It looked just like a colourful and celebratory wedding procession.

'What is going on?' Jan asked.

I asked the driver and he confirmed what I had thought. We had stumbled upon an exhumation ceremony, which traditionally took place in September/October, in the dry season. We were very lucky, the driver said, as exhumation ceremonies normally happened in remote areas, so it was unusual to come upon them. We watched the procession disappear into the distance; it was spooky, yet interesting at the same time. The thought of those dead bodies passing in front of my eyes made me feel a little strange, uncomfortable; but then again it was a custom that deserved to be respected.

The driver explained that the purpose of the ritual was to reunite people with their families again, appease their ancestors, and honour their dead. Their relationships were never truly over; they would always keep their connection alive. It was truly a memorable experience and one that will stay with me always. That was what I loved about Madagascar: the mixture of the modern and the old—state-of-the-art computer systems, cell phones, TV; and the old ways, religion and respect for tradition.

In February 2008 I went down to Fort Dauphin on the southeast coast to have some meetings before the rest of the consultants arrived. It was there that we were to continue with the next phase of our project. I had heard tales of how remote it was, how careful you had to be with what you ate, and the almost constant power issues, so I was apprehensive. I was due to stay for four days, together with Hery, one of my colleagues. He had often been to Fort Dauphin so he would be able to show me around and give me a good orientation.

We arrived on a glorious day, hot and sunny but not too humid; the wind was just blowing slightly, swaying the palm trees. We drove from the airport to the main offices in town past scenes of grinding poverty.

The roads were dusty and potholed, with most of the dwellings being shacks on the hillsides. I had heard there was very little sanitation, which was why so many people just squatted by the roadside when they needed to relieve themselves.

The open-air market was abuzz with people dressed in clothes that hung in rags, washed endless times until most of the colour had faded. In between were people with brightly coloured clothes, obviously employed, and with a little more money to spend. Despite the poverty and obvious difficulties of life, most people we drove past had cheery smiles, happy enough, it seemed, with their lot.

The next few days went by quickly. Hery left Fort Dauphin earlier than I, so I had some time on Saturday morning to explore. The driver said he would take me out to the beach and the lakes and give me a general understanding of the area. It was a truly beautiful environment: palm trees, dunes, and clear blue sea, a tropical Indian Ocean paradise. We parked for a while near one of the lakes, watching the dugout canoes being paddled out by local fishermen to check their shrimp nets. Those that came back smiled at us. Their clothes were ragged and they were painfully thin.

'Are they content with their lives?' I asked the driver. 'It must be such a hard life. Do they ever move to Tana to earn more money?'

He looked at me, surprised at my question. 'Why wouldn't they be happy, and content? They fish, they feed their families, then they sell whatever is left over to buy rice and clothes. What more do they need?'

Indeed, what more do they need? I felt humbled by this response. Here I was, imposing my first-world standards of consumerism. What right did I have to think that having more money would bring more happiness? It was presumptuous of me. Life in Fort Dauphin was simpler, probably less stressful, and had a lot to offer in its own particular way— as I found out when I returned for the last part of the project.

In March we were ready for "go-live" and were to start the training

Fort Dauphin

in the mine admin buildings that had just been built. The mine itself was not yet functional. It had been raining for days as a cyclone passed to the north of the island. Anita had just flown in to provide support during this crucial period. We chatted easily over dinner at Coco Beach, looking out to the lake and enjoying the coolness of the evening.

Anita had read my book. 'It was such a fascinating story', she said, 'but I battled to relate the strong independent person I know with the person in the book, you seem miles apart'. It was true, I thought to myself, I was a different person, I had left the old Mary far behind. It was good to hear Anita's comments; I realised that in many ways, John's leaving me had done me so much good. It had made me who I am today. I was experiencing amazing things, making a life for myself, and I appreciated that. Of course when it was all happening that was the last thing I felt, confused and vulnerable as I was. But look at me now, a book under my belt, a screenplay in progress, and work that brought me the opportunity to experience so many amazing things!

As the days went on the rains got worse and worse, to the extent that in our first days of training, we had to evacuate the mine as there was a fear that one of the newly constructed bridges on the route between town and the mine might collapse. We were at the mercy of the elements and the experience made me realise how vulnerable we would always be. No matter how strong and in control we felt, something could always conspire to knock us off balance. We survived the near-cyclone and life continued to move along—tough deadlines, lots of meetings. It was challenging, but also fun and rewarding as things gradually started to come together and people started to use the system.

It wasn't all hard work, though. There were memorable spontaneous moments when a few of us ended up down at the beach at Ancuba. One Saturday afternoon, Andry brought his guitar and we bumped into other colleagues—Hery, Onja, Bertrand, Sandra, Tsila—had lunch together, and then sat on the beach afterwards as Andry played and the others sang

Saturday afternoon at Ancuba Beach

along, traditional Madagascan songs and some English ones too. We sat in a circle, which grew bigger and bigger as more and more people joined us. We were a mixture of so many nationalities united through music. We sat back in the sand under the palm trees, looking out to sea, and our voices rose together as we found harmony through song. It

Madagascar Beach

was magical, hanging out on our tropical island. Madagascar was all about simplicity: a guitar and some friends, what more did we need?

The highlight of Sundays in Fort Dauphin was generally a visit to Miramar for brunch. This would often become the main outing of the weekend. I waited at the Hotel du Phare with the other consultants from Mauritius for Niry to collect us in the minibus. Niry was our driver; he was young and tall, with a ready smile and gentle manner. He was always willing to go out of his way to help us, teaching himself English to make it easier to deal with the visitors that came to the mine from Australia and South Africa. Niry's minibus was always spotless and he took pride in his position as a driver. So diligent was he that he became the supervisor of the other drivers, organising their daily schedules.

Niry greeted us that morning as we climbed into the minibus. It was a beautiful morning, clear blue skies, not too humid, with a light breeze. It promised to be a stunning day. I had been up since early, taking a walk to 6 AM Mass (the services were early to escape the heat of the day), and I had already done some work on my screenplay. Brunch would be a nice break before continuing with my writing. I had almost finished the screenplay, and was anxious to finalise it before I left the island for good.

Niry explained that we had to make a detour via Ancuba Beach. Robert Mills, our project sponsor, had gone there to surf and needed to be picked up so that he could join us for brunch. We lurched down the narrow gravel road, avoiding scrawny chickens running out in front of us, passing children carrying containers of water on their heads, and weaving from side to side to avoid the potholes. The minibus had to stop above the beach—we needed a 4x4 vehicle to get down there. Niry phoned Robert to tell him we had arrived. Robert made his way up the hill, his surfboard under his arm. Born in England, with an Irish mother, but now based in the States, he was tall and lanky, with a mop of unruly hair and a dry sense of humour.

Robert eased the surfboard into the minibus and greeted us all. I had always wanted to surf; it was on my never-ending list of things to do in life. I kept working my way through them, but the more I ticked off the more I added. I just loved trying new things.

'I'd love to learn to surf', I said to Robert. "But I'm thinking it may be too late now.' I was aware of how little time I had left in Madagascar.

'Nonsense', he replied. 'You're not too old to learn, it's never too late.'

I laughed. 'I wasn't meaning I was too old, I meant I didn't know if I would be able to fit it in, considering the time I have left here.'

Robert looked uncomfortable. 'Oh dear', he said. 'I've put my foot in it, haven't I?'

I smiled reassuringly. 'Don't worry, I am only a couple of years older than you and I know I can do it. Age is certainly not the issue.'

Robert's faux pas became a standing joke between us. It's never too late to try something new, that is for sure. I have so much I still want to do, nothing will stop me now. I was in a privileged place, the world at my feet and not an obstacle in sight.

It was nearly time for me to leave Madagascar; although the original contract of a few months had turned into a much longer stay, my year there had flown by. It was a sad day when the time finally came for me to leave.

'The driver is waiting for you', one of my colleagues said. I was busy saying my goodbyes to the people I had worked with. My year there had been an exciting time for me, difficult and very trying at times, but I had made good friends and was sad to leave. I was surprised by just how emotional I was becoming. It was hard to say goodbye to people I had worked so closely with, lived with, and socialised with. We had been on a long journey together and had supported each other along the way.

I couldn't continue saying my goodbyes any longer. I had to go to the minibus before I made a complete fool of myself in front of everyone. I dabbed at my eyes with a tissue and bolted for the minibus. Niry smiled as he opened the door. I kept my head down, trying to stop him spotting the tears streaming down my face. There was another person in the mini-bus, someone senior from Canada; I sat behind him, trying to compose myself. I didn't want to make a fool of myself in front of a complete stranger. Finally I succeeded in stopping the tears. Hopefully Niry would start the engine soon and we could be on our way.

I looked out of the window at the mine buildings and over to the hills on the other side. Just at that moment, Bertrand, the Canadian finance manager, came running out to say his goodbyes. He had been a good friend during my time there and had heard that I was upset. He was concerned and wanted to check that I was OK. Bertrand's kind words set me off again. He spoke to the other passenger, whom he knew well from the time they had worked together in Canada.

'Look after Mary', he said. 'She is very dear to us.'

With that, Niry started the bus and we set off for the airport. My travelling companion was very kind, chatting to me about the project I had just finished in Madagascar, trying to keep my mind off my sadness at saying goodbye. The twenty-minute drive went by very quickly. I had now composed myself to a certain extent. All that remained was to check in at the little airport and then say goodbye to Niry.

We stopped in the dusty parking area and Niry helped me with my case. He carried it over to the customs table, where I would have to open it for the customs officials. Niry asked me to see him after I checked in. Very little was automated here; it was just a big room, with fans forlornly trying to reduce the still, humid heat inside the building.

Once the customs formalities were over I wheeled my case to the check-in counter. I crossed my fingers that my luggage would not be over the fifteen-kilo limit, as I had bought a few last-minute presents. It was OK; I had just made it. I picked up my handwritten boarding card, detailing that I was the fifteenth passenger to check in. There was no seat number on it. It was every man for himself once the plane arrived. I didn't mind—I was generally one of only one or two women on the plane, and was often shown the courtesy of being let on in front of the men. I went outside to find Niry.

He was standing next to the minibus, looking forlorn. I walked over to him and as I held his gaze, both our eyes misted over. Niry was naturally shy, and hesitated a moment before starting to speak. I realised that he had prepared a speech for me; this was not off the cuff, it had been carefully thought out and rehearsed. Niry straightened himself up, looked at me with a steady gaze and started to speak. He thanked me for all the support and guidance I had given him. He had progressed in his job because of my guidance, and he wanted to thank me and let me know how special I was. He had no gift for me, but I should know that his wish was for me to return to Madagascar. He asked me to keep in touch and gave me his email address.

I was so touched; Niry's speech was beautiful and had come straight from his heart. I had done very little for him, yet it had meant so much. His appreciation meant so much more to me than any corporate accolade could have. If only I can continue to touch people's hearts and minds like this, I will be happy. I shook Niry's hand, smiling at him through my tears, and went through to the departure lounge.

I realised that Madagascar had taught me many things, far more than I had taught anybody there. It had made me appreciate the value of a simple, uncluttered life, and I vowed to endeavour to simplify my own life on my return to South Africa. The people were open and honest, with a friendliness and spontaneity I loved. I made incredible friends there, and knew that wherever I would go in the future, Madagascar would hold a particular place in my heart. It had given me perspective when I truly needed it, giving me the space and environment in which to reflect on where I was in life and what had changed since I had written my first book.

I had never anticipated the journey that my book would trigger. Writing it had opened my life to scrutiny, to question. I could no longer shy away from confronting issues as people delved into my personal life. *Remember Me?* had led me back to John and the closing of that chapter of my life. I can honestly say that I have followed the advice contained in my mother's journal: *I hope you both will too, always be true to yourselves.*

As I write this second book, involved as I am in a variety of things for which I have a passion, I realise how my life has moved on. I am truly my own person, happy in my own skin. My journey to find John was ultimately also a journey to find myself.

'Who do you belong to?'

Would anyone think of asking me that question now? I think not.